VOCAL / PIANO

ACROSS THE UNIVERSE

ORIGINAL KEYS FOR SINGERS

ISBN 978-1-4234-6048-0

HOLD ME TIGHT

Words and Music by JOHN LENNON
and PAUL McCARTNEY

D7
G
lone - ly one. So, hold me tight
G7
C
Cm
to - night, to - night. It's
G
Cm
G
you; you, you, you.
N.C.
G
1.,3., Hold me tight;
2. Hold me tight;

C7 A7

let me go on
tell me I'm the

D7 G

lov - ing you to - night, to - night,
on - ly one, and then I might

C7 A7

mak - ing love to
nev - er be the

D7 G

on - ly you. So, hold me tight
lone - ly one.

C
to - night,
to -
Cm
- night.
It's
G
you;
Cm
To Coda
you,
you,
G
you
B♭5
don't
G5
know
B♭5
what it means
to
G5
hold you tight,
C5
be - ing here a -

N.C.
lone to - night with you. It
1
2
D.S. al Coda
feels so right, now. feels so right, now.
CODA
G
B♭5
G5
you,
B♭5
G5
G6
ooh.
rit.

ALL MY LOVING

Words and Music by JOHN LENNON
and PAUL McCARTNEY

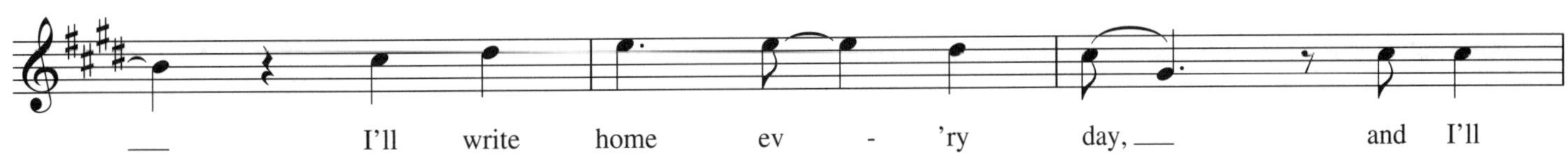

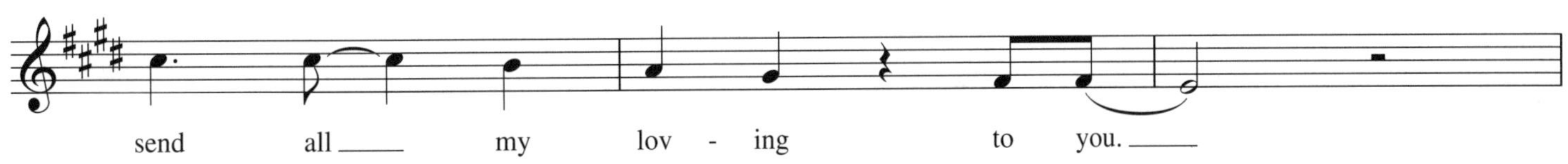

Moderate Shuffle
F♯m
B
E
I'll pre - tend that I'm kiss - ing the lips I am
and I'll kiss you; to - mor - row, I'll
mf
C♯m
F♯m7
F♯m
miss - ing, and hope that my dreams will come
miss you. Re - mem - ber, I'll al - ways be
D
B
F♯m
B
true.
true.
And then while I'm a - way, I'll write
E
C♯m
F♯m7
home ev - 'ry day, and I'll send all my

B
E
C♯m
lov- ing
to
you.
All
my
lov- ing,
I
C+
E/B
E+
will
send
to
you.
All
my
To Coda
C♯m
C+
E/B
E
lov- ing;
dar
-
ling, I'll
be
true.
Instrumental solo
F♯m7
B
E
C♯m

F♯m7
B
E
D.S. al Coda
Solo ends Close your eyes
CODA
C♯m
All my lov - ing,
C+
E/B
E+
all my lov - ing,
all my
C♯m
C+
E/B
E
lov - ing
I will send to you.

I WANT TO HOLD YOUR HAND

Words and Music by JOHN LENNON
and PAUL McCARTNEY

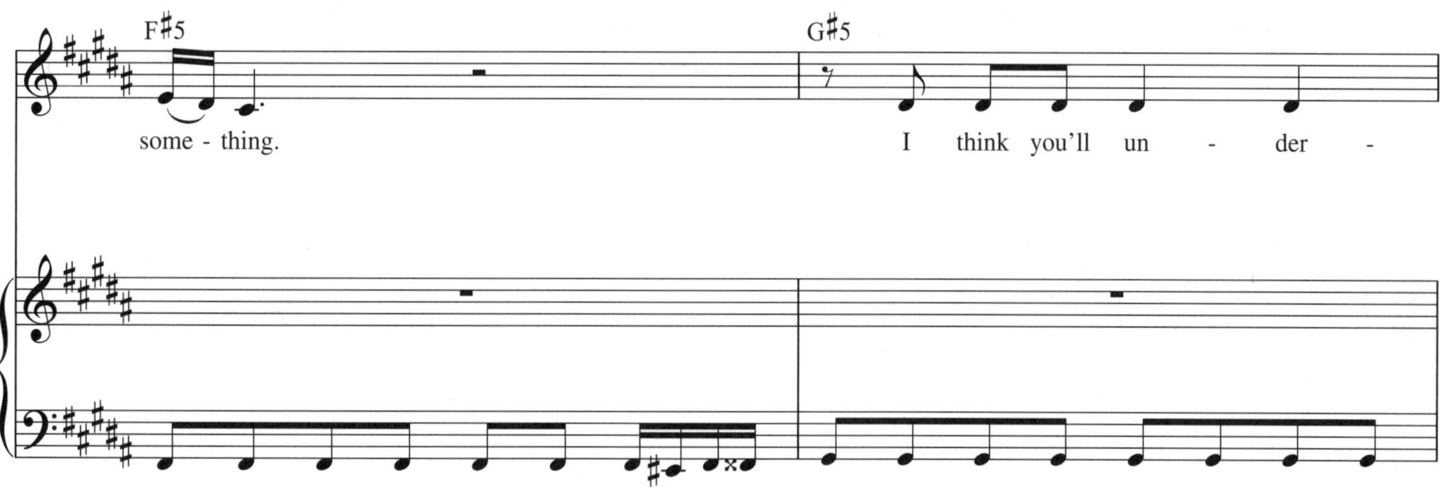

F♯5
G♯5
some - thing:
I want to hold your hand.
D♯5
E5
F♯5
I want to hold your
B5
G♯5
E5
F♯5
hand.
I want to hold your
B5
Bsus2
hand.
Oh
please
say to

F♯sus2 G♯m7

me you'll let me be your

D♯5 Bsus2

man. And please say to

F♯sus2 G♯m7

me you'll let me hold your hand.

Bsus2
G♯m11
Esus2
F♯sus2
hand.
I want to hold your
Bsus2
F♯m(add2)
B5
hand.
And when I touch you I feel
E5
C♯5
F♯5
hap - py in - side.
It's such a feel -
B5
E5
F♯5
E5
- ing that my love I can't hide, I can't

F♯5
E5
F♯5
hide, I can't hide. Yeah,
Bsus2
F♯sus2
you, you've got that some - thing,
G♯m7
D♯5
I think you'll un - der - stand. When
Bsus2
F♯(add2)
I feel that some - thing,

G♯m7
D♯5
I want to hold your hand.
Esus2
F♯sus
Bsus2
G♯m11
I want to hold your hand.
Esus2
F♯(add4)
D♯5
I want to hold your hand.
Emaj7
F♯5
E5
E/G♯
F♯sus
E5
E/G♯
F♯sus
B6/9
I want to hold your hand.
rit.
3
3
3
3

WITH A LITTLE HELP FROM MY FRIENDS

Words and Music by JOHN LENNON
and PAUL McCARTNEY

F♯m(add♭2)
B
you a song, and I'll try not to sing out of key.
E(add♯9)
D
A
Oh, I get by with a lit - tle help from my friends.
E
D
A
II: (Gets high with a lit - tle help from his friends.)
E
A9
I: Oh, I'm gon-na try, with a lit - tle help from my friends.

E(add♯9)
B
I: What do I do when my love
F♯m(add♭2)
B
is a - way? II: Does it wor - ry you to be a - lone?
E(add♯9)
E(add♯9)
B
I: How do I feel by the end
F♯m(add♭2)
B
of the day? II: Are you sad be - cause you're on your own?

E(add♯9)
D
A
Both:
I: I get by with a lit - tle help from my friends.
E
D
A
Both:
II: Yeah, I get high with a lit - tle help from my friends.
E(add♯9)
A/D
Both:
I: Oh, I'm gon - na try, with a lit - tle help from my friends.
E
C♯m
II: Do you need an - y - bod -

C♯m/F♯
E
D
- y?
I: I
need
some - bod - y
to
love. _
A
C♯m
II: Could
it
be
an - y - bod -
C♯m/F♯
E
D
A
- y?
I: I
want
some - bod - y
to
love.
E
B
F♯m7
Both: Would
you
be - lieve
in
a
love
at
first
sight?
II: Yeah,
I'm

B5/F♯
E
cer - tain that it hap - pens all the time.
B
F♯m7
Both: What do you see when you turn out the light? I: I can't tell
B5/F♯
E
you, but I know it's mine. Oh, I get by
Both:
D
A
E
with a lit - tle help from my friends. Mmm, I get high

D
A
E
with a lit - tle help from my friends.
Oh, I'm gon-na try
A7
E
B5
A5
F♯5
with a lit - tle help from my friends.
A5
G5/D
G5
E5
Do you need an - y - bod - y?
D5
B5
A5
F♯5
I: I need some-one to love.

A5
Both: Could it be an - y - bod - y?
G5/D
G5
E5
B
Whoa,
whoa.
B7
N.C.
D
By
Try
with a lit - tle help from my
Asus2

E
D
Asus2
friends.
By with a lit - tle help from my
1
2
friends.
friends.
Expressively
D
A
I: I get by with a lit - tle help from my friends, with a lit - tle
Moderately slow
C/G
F♯m7♭5
E
help from my friends.
rit.
8vb

IT WON'T BE LONG

Words and Music by JOHN LENNON
and PAUL McCARTNEY

E♭5
G5
Ev - 'ry night, when ev - 'ry - bod - y has fun,
E♭5
G5
here am I, sit - ting all on my own.
2, 3
G
It won't be
Since you left me,
F♯+
F6
E7
I'm so a - lone. Now you're com - ing, you're com - ing on home.

C
D7
A7
3
I'll be good like I know I should. You're com - ing home, you're com - ing
D7
G5
E♭5
home.
Ev - 'ry night the tears come down from my
Ev - 'ry day, we'll be hap - py, I
G5
To Coda
eyes.
know.
Ev - 'ry day,
E♭5
G5
D.S. al Coda
(take 3rd ending)
I've done noth - ing but cry.
It won't be

CODA
Eb5
G5
Now I know that you won't leave me no more.
Em
(It won't be long, yeah), yeah, (yeah), yeah, (yeah), yeah. (It won't be
G
Em
long, yeah), yeah, (yeah), yeah, (yeah), yeah. (It won't be long, yeah), yeah, 'til
Slowly, freely
C
C♯dim7
G5
I be - long to you.

I'VE JUST SEEN A FACE

Words and Music by JOHN LENNON
and PAUL McCARTNEY

Em

met. She's just the girl ___ for me, and I ___
I'd have nev - er been ___ a - ware. But as ___
missed things and kept ___ out of sight, but oth -

___ want all the world ___ to see we've
___ it is, I'll dream ___ of her to -
- er girls were ___ nev - er quite like

Csus2

met. Mmm, mmm,
night. Di, di,
this. Mmm, mmm,

D5 | 1 G5 | 2, 3 G5

mmm, mmm, mmm, mmm. ___
di, di, di, di. ___ ___
mmm, mmm, mmm, mmm. _ ___

Dsus2
Csus2
Fall - ing, yes, I am fall - ing,
and she keeps call - ing
G5
To Coda
C5
me back a - gain.
G5
D.S. al Coda
(Take 3rd ending)
CODA
C5
me back a - gain.
G5
G5
Guitar solos ad lib.

G5/F♯

Em

Csus2

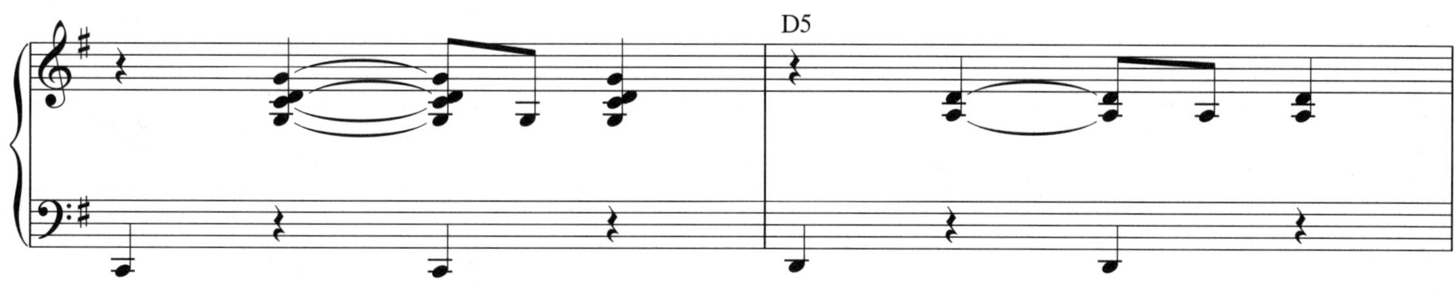
D5

1
G5
2

Dsus2
Csus2
(1., 2.) Fall - ing, yes, I am fall - ing,
(3.) (Fall - ing, yes, he is fall - ing),
and she keeps call - ing
G5
1, 2
C5
me back a - gain.
G5
3
C5
me back a - gain.
G5
D5
G

LET IT BE

Words and Music by JOHN LENNON
and PAUL McCARTNEY

Freely, with a Gospel feel

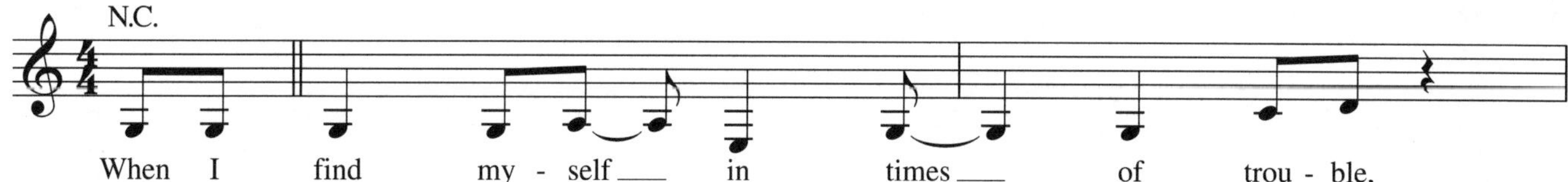

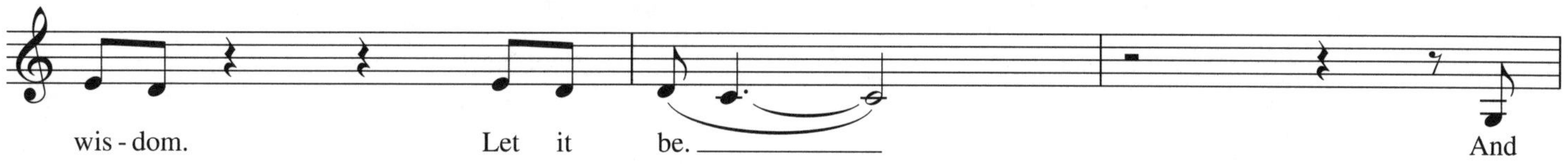

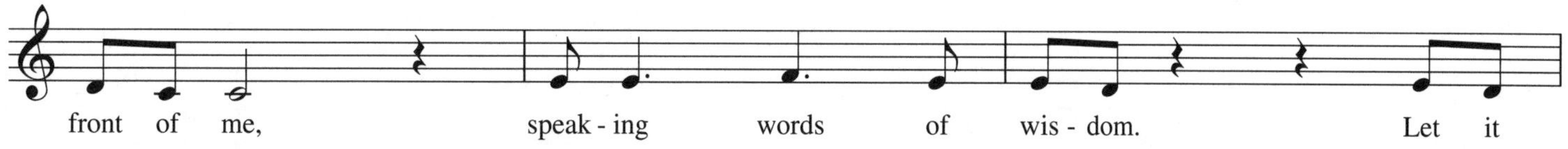

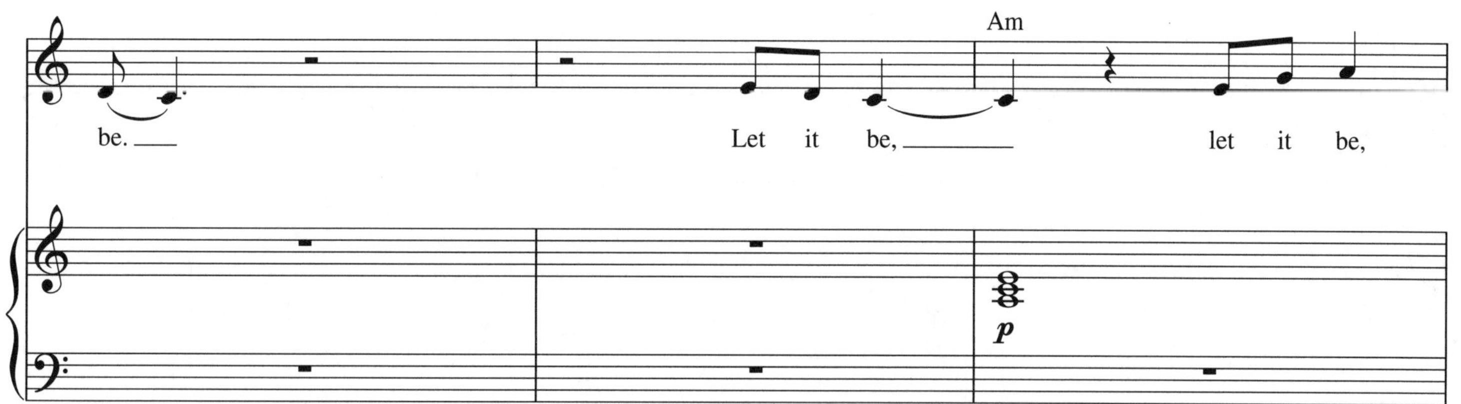

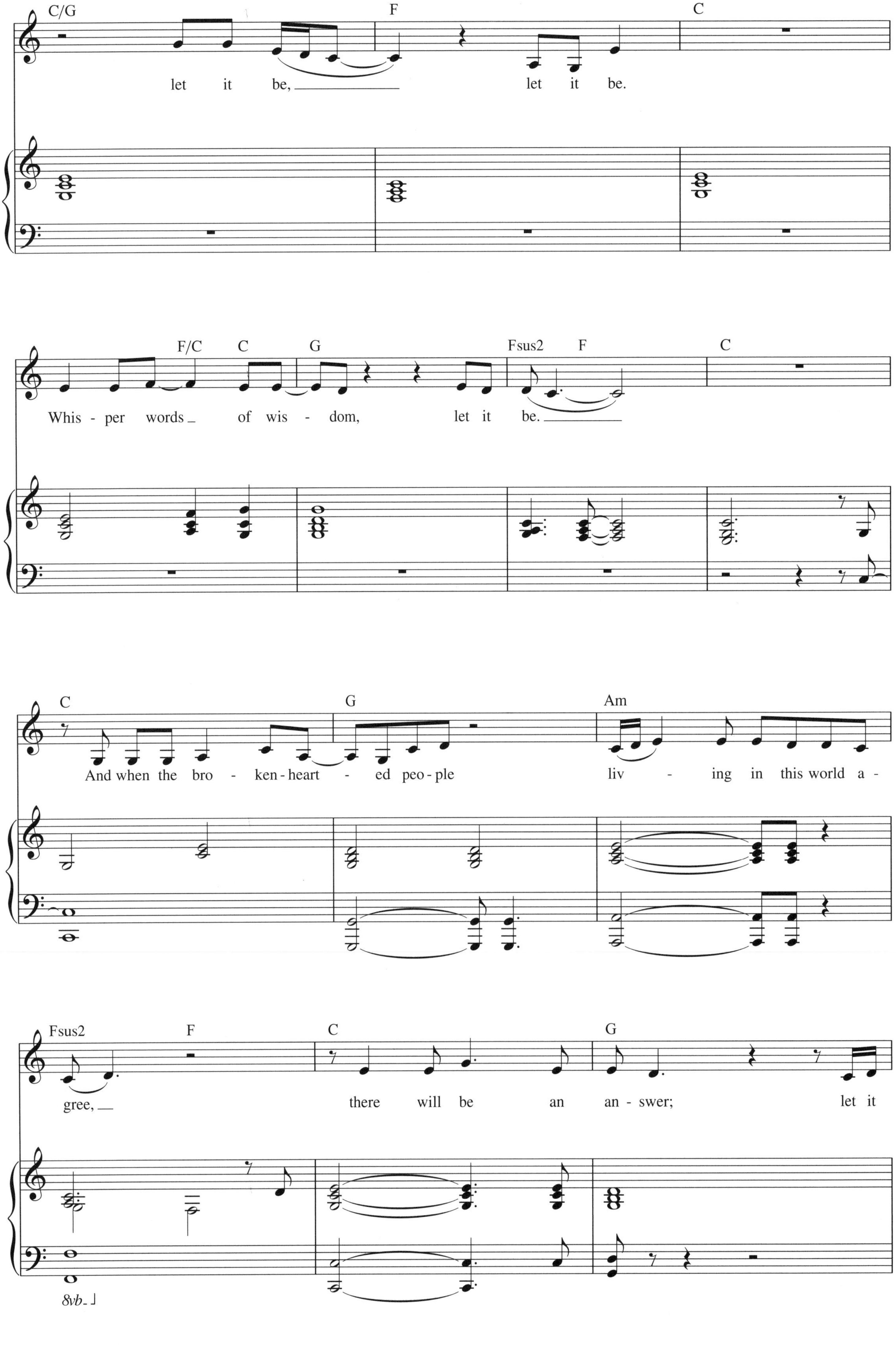

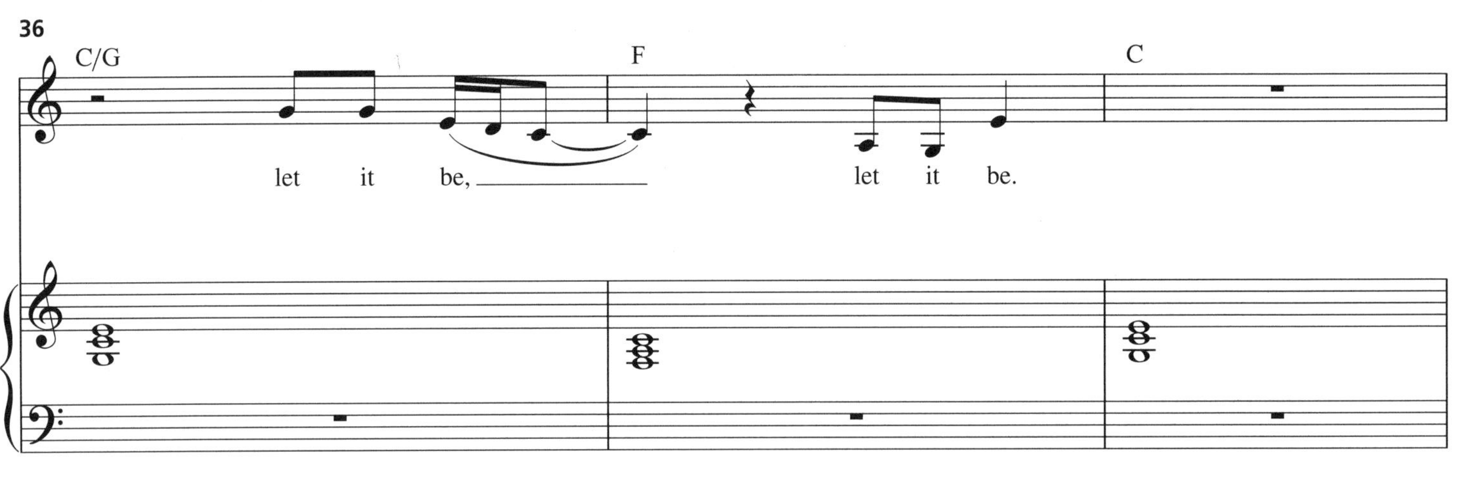

C G Am

And when the bro - ken - heart - ed peo - ple liv - ing in this world a -

Fsus2 F C G

gree, there will be an an - swer; let it

8vb

F
C
be.
For though they may be
8vb
G
Am
Fmaj9
Dm/G
part - ed,
there is still a chance that they will see.
C
Dm
C/E
G
F
C/E
Dm7
(There will be an an - swer, let it be.)
8vb
C
Am
C/G
Let it be, let it be, let it
(8vb)

Fmaj7 F6 C Dm7/C C Dm C/E
be, let it be. (There will be an an -
G F C/E Dm7 C
- swer, let it be.) Oh,
Am Am/A♭ Am/G C/G Fmaj7 F/G
let it be, let it be, let it be, let it
C F/C C Dm/C C Dm C/E G
be. (Whis - per words of wis - dom, let it
8vb

F C/E Dm7 C
be.) And when the night is cloud -
(8vb)
G6 G Am F
- y, there is still a light that shines on me.
C G Fsus2
Shine un - til to - mor - row, let it be.
C/F C Dm C/E G
I wake up to the sound of mu - sic.

Am7 Fmaj9 C Dm C/E

Moth - er Ma - ry, Moth - er Ma - ry comes to me, (speak - ing words of wis -

G F C/E Dm7 C Gsus

- dom, let it be.)

Am A♭+ C/G C/F Dm/G F/G

(Let it be, let it be, let it be.

C Dm7 C/E C Dm/C C6 G

Oh, there will be an an - swer, let it

F C/E Dm7 C Am7
be.) Let it be (let it be), Let it
8vb
C/G C/F C Dm/C C Dm/C
be (let it be), Let it be (let it be), let it be.
Slowly, freely
C G F
Whis-per words of wis-dom, let it be.
C F C/E Dm C B♭ F/A E♭sus2/G
rit.

COME TOGETHER

Words and Music by JOHN LENNON
and PAUL McCARTNEY

N.C.
Got to be a jok - er, he just do what he please.
He wear no shoe - shine; he got toe - jam foot - ball; he got
He bag pro - duc - tion; he got wal - rus gum - boot; he got
He roll - er coast - er; he got ear - ly warn - ing; he got
G5
mon - key fin - ger; he shoot Co - ca Co - la. He say, "I know you,
o - no side - board; he one spin - al crack - er. He got feet down be - low
mud - dy wat - er; he one mo - jo fil - ter. He say, "One and one and one

N.C.
you know me.
his knees.
is three."
One thing I can tell you is you
Hold you in his arm - chair, you can
Got to be good - look - ing, 'cause he's
A5
G5
got to be free."
feel his dis - ease.
so hard to see.
Come to - geth - er right
F5
G5
N.C.
To Coda
now o - ver me.
2nd time: Instrumental solo ad lib.

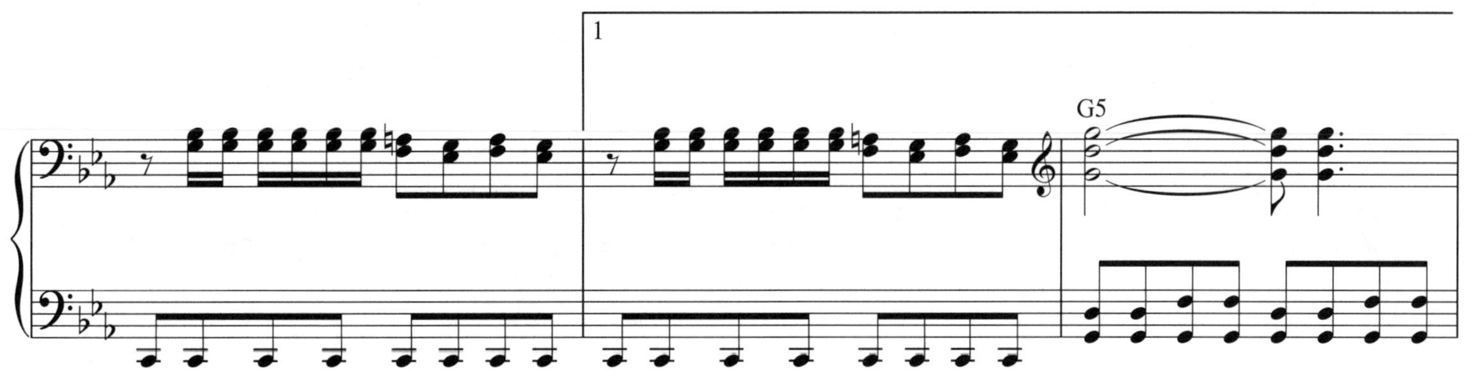
1
G5

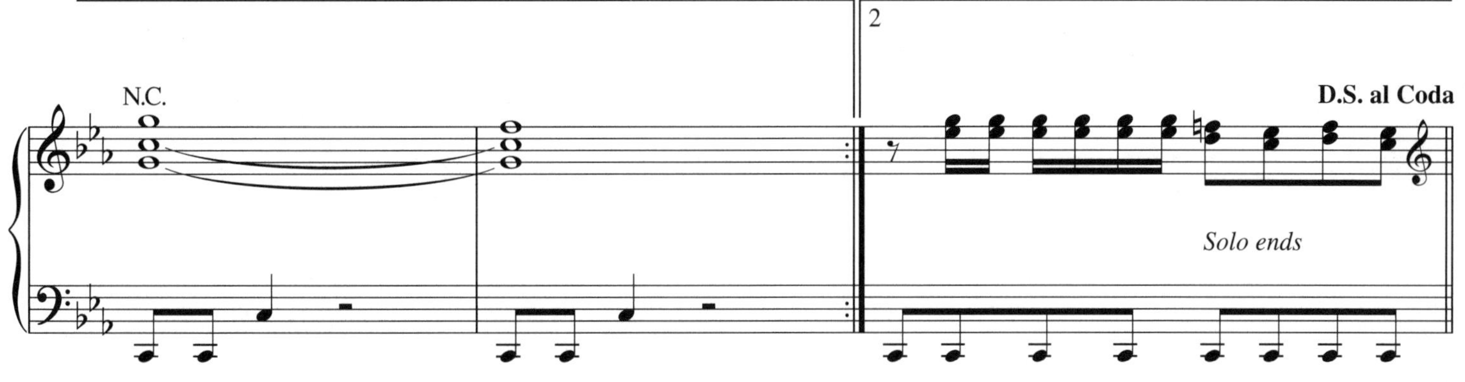
N.C.
2
D.S. al Coda
Solo ends

CODA
O - ver me.

Come to-geth - er.
Yeah.
Vocal continues ad lib.

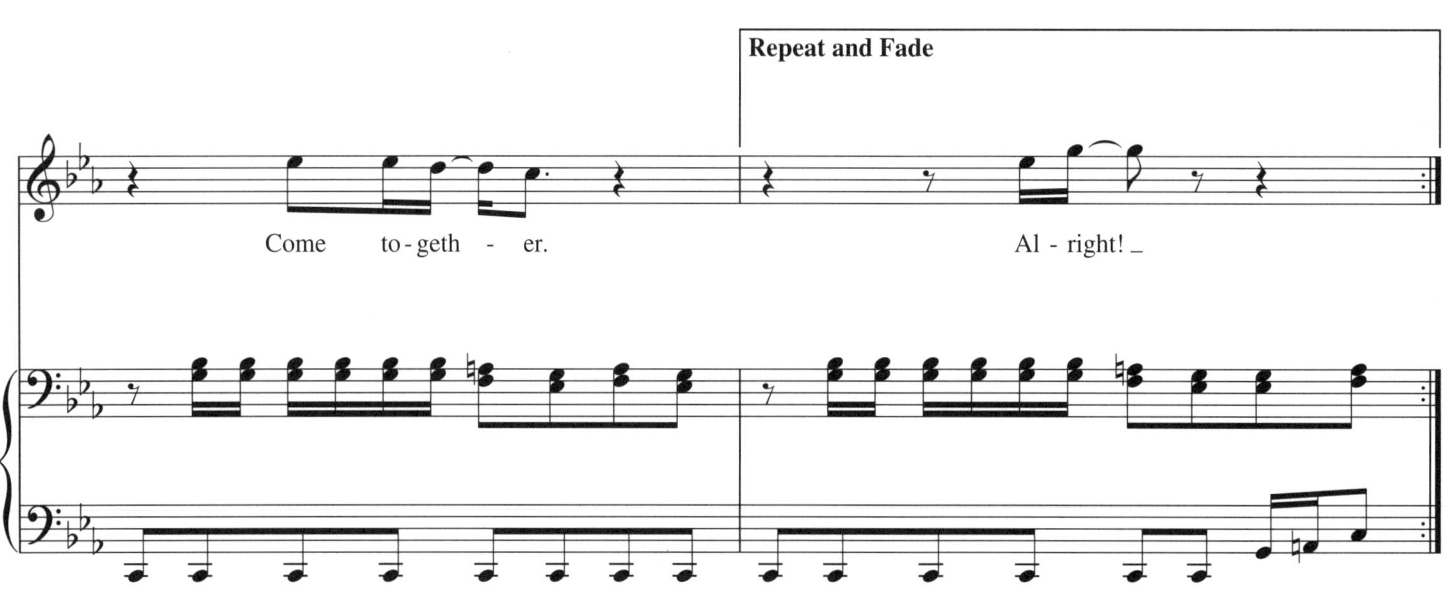
Repeat and Fade
Come to-geth - er.
Al - right!

Optional Ending

I AM THE WALRUS

Words and Music by JOHN LENNON
and PAUL McCARTNEY

C5
D5
See how they run, like pigs from a gun, see how they fly. I'm
A5
N.C.
cry - in'.
Sit-ting on a corn - flake,
wait-ing for the van to come.
F(add2)/C
B7
Cor-po-ra-tion t-shirt, stu-pid blood-y Tues-day, man, you've been a naugh-ty boy, you let your face grow

C7
long.
I am the Egg - man;
they are the
D7
E
Egg - men;
I am the wal - rus.
Goo goo g' - joob.
A5
G5
C5
D5
Mis - ter Cit - y po - lice - man sit - ting
pret - ty lit - tle po - lice - men in a row.
A5
G5
C5
See how they fly, like Lu - cy in the sky, see

D5
A5
how they run.
I'm cry - in'.
Dsus
I'm
N.C.
E
cry - in',
cry -
D5
N.C.
- in'.
Yel - low mat - ter cus - tard

drip-ping from a dead dog's eye.
F(add2)
Crab - a - lock - er fish - wife, por - no - graph - ic priest - ess, boy,
B5
you've been a naugh - ty girl, you let your knick-ers down.
I am the
C7
Egg - man;
they are the
D7
Egg - men;
I am the

E
N.C.
wal - rus. Go goo g'-joob.
E
B5
A5
Gmaj7(no3rd)
F♯m7(add4)
Sit - ting in an Eng - lish gar - den wait - ing for the sun.
E
B7
If the sun don't come, you get a tan from stand - ing in the Eng - lish

C7
rain.
I am the Egg - man; they are the
D7
E
Egg - men; I am the wal - rus. Goo goo g' - joob, g - goo
D
C7
goo g' joob. Goo goo g' - joob, g - goo goo g' joob.
D
A5
G5
Ex - pert, tex - pert, chok - ing smok - ers,

C5
D5
A5
G5
don't you think the jok - er laughs at you?
C5
D5
See how they smile, like pigs in a sty, see how they snide. I'm
A5
N.C.
cry - in'. Sem - o - li - na Pil - chard
climb-ing up the Eif - fel Tow - er.

F(add2)
El - e - men - t'ry pen - guin sing - ing Ha - re Krish - na, man,
B5
you should have seen them kick - ing Ed - gar Al - lan Poe.
I am the
C7
Egg - man;
they are the
D7
Egg - men;
I am the
E
wal - rus.
Goo goo g' - joob, g - goo
D
goo g' joob.

C7
B(add4)
Goo goo g'-joob, g - goo — goo g'-joob.
N.C.
Ju - ba, ju - ba, ju - ba, jub ju - ba! Ju - ba.
Jub ju - ba, ju - ba, ju - ba. Jub ju - ba! Come on, jub, ju - ba.
Spoken: Three the farm Wayne skies. Rippin' at the blues! You know; it's true.

Sharin' eggs were there before I make you.
(Various sound effects...)
Nice.
Love the people.
Love the people.
Love the people.
Love the people.
Love the people.
(Vocal and sound effects continue ad lib.)
Repeat and Fade
Optional Ending

BECAUSE

Words and Music by JOHN LENNON
and PAUL McCARTNEY

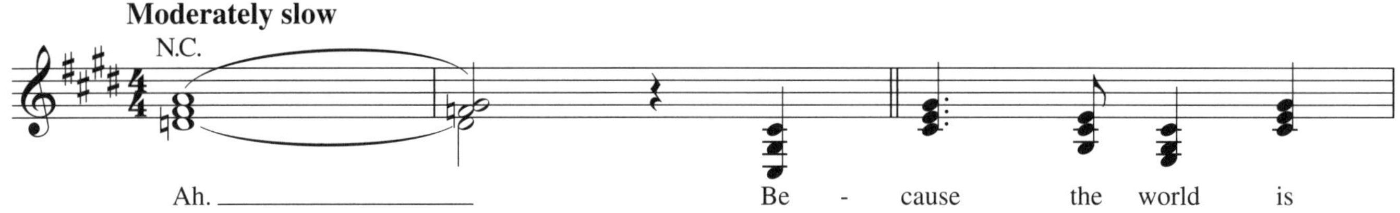

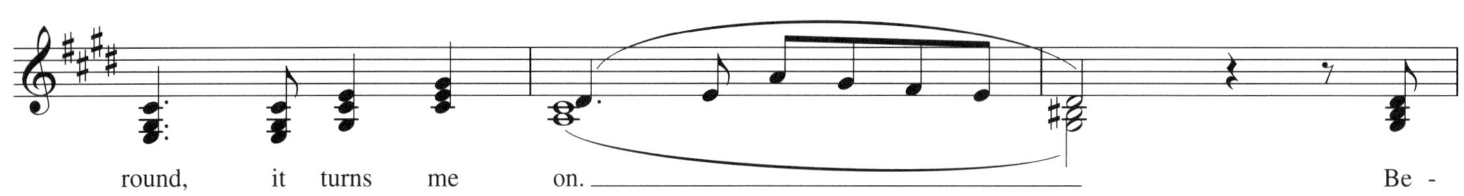

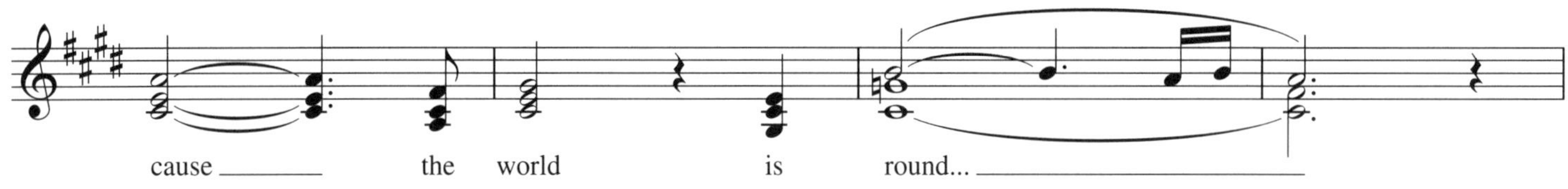

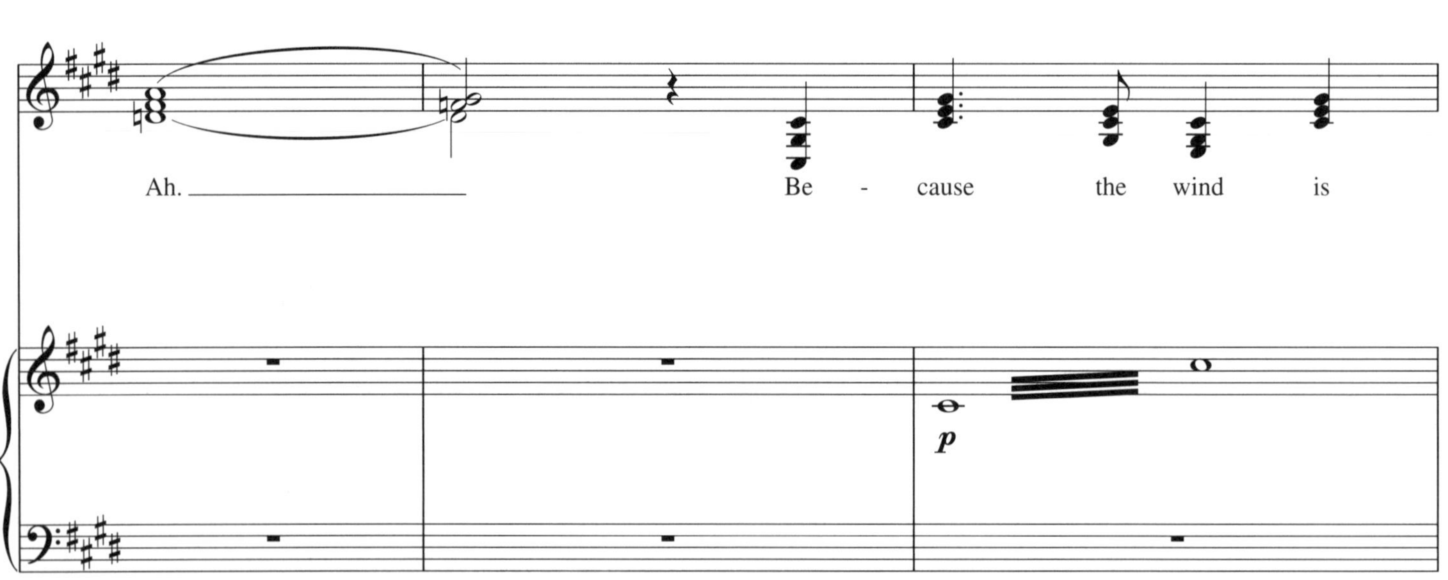

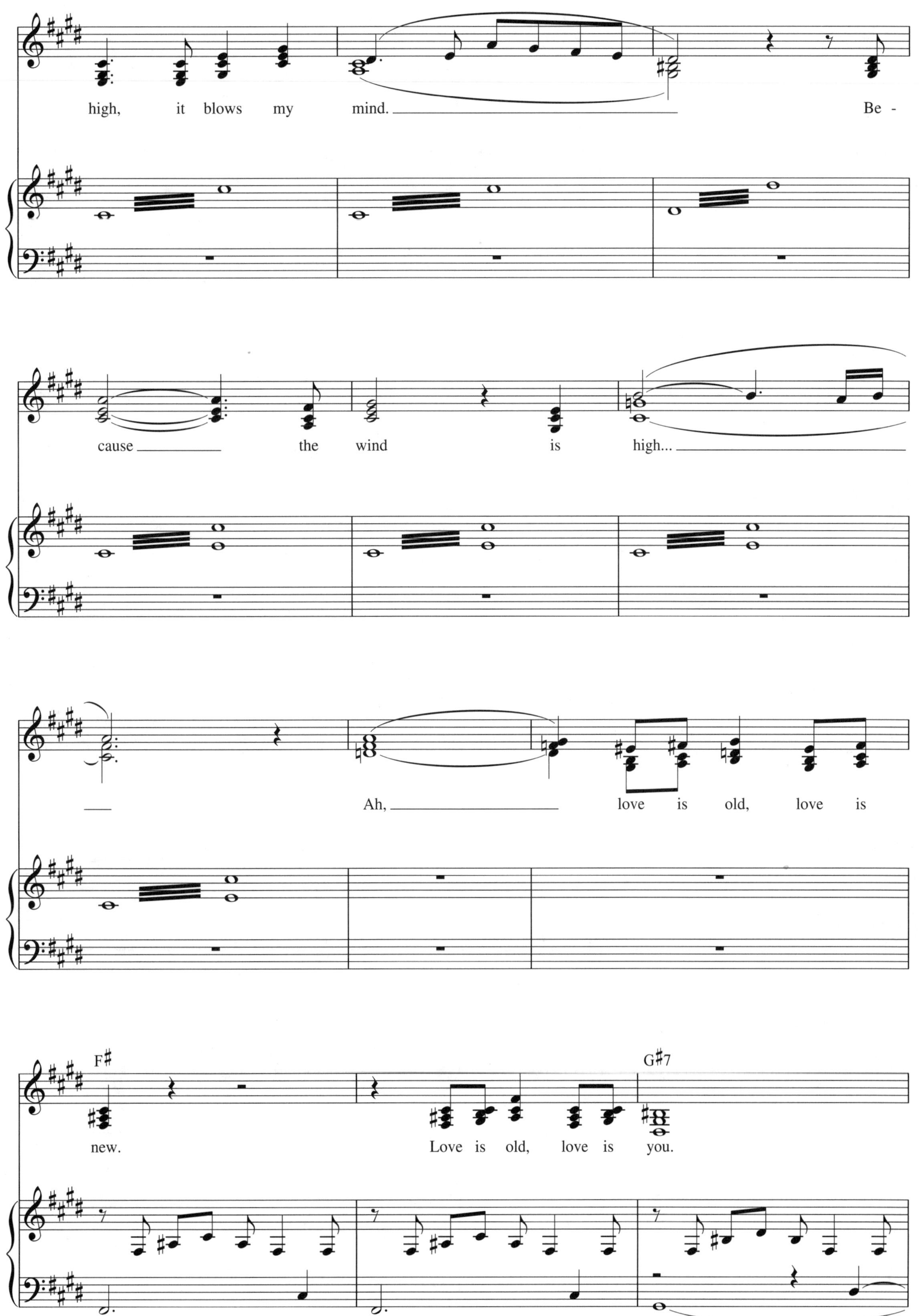
high, it blows my mind. Be -
cause the wind is high...
Ah, love is old, love is
F♯
new. Love is old, love is you.
G♯7

C♯m
Be - cause the sky is blue, it makes me
D♯m7♭5
D♯m7♭5/A
G♯
A
cry.
Be - cause the
C♯m
A7
3
sky is blue...
A13
D
Ah.

Ddim7
C♯m
D♯m7♭5
D♯m7♭5/A
G♯
A
Ah.
C♯m
A7
3
Ah.
A13
D
Ddim7
Ah.

SOMETHING

Words and Music by
GEORGE HARRISON

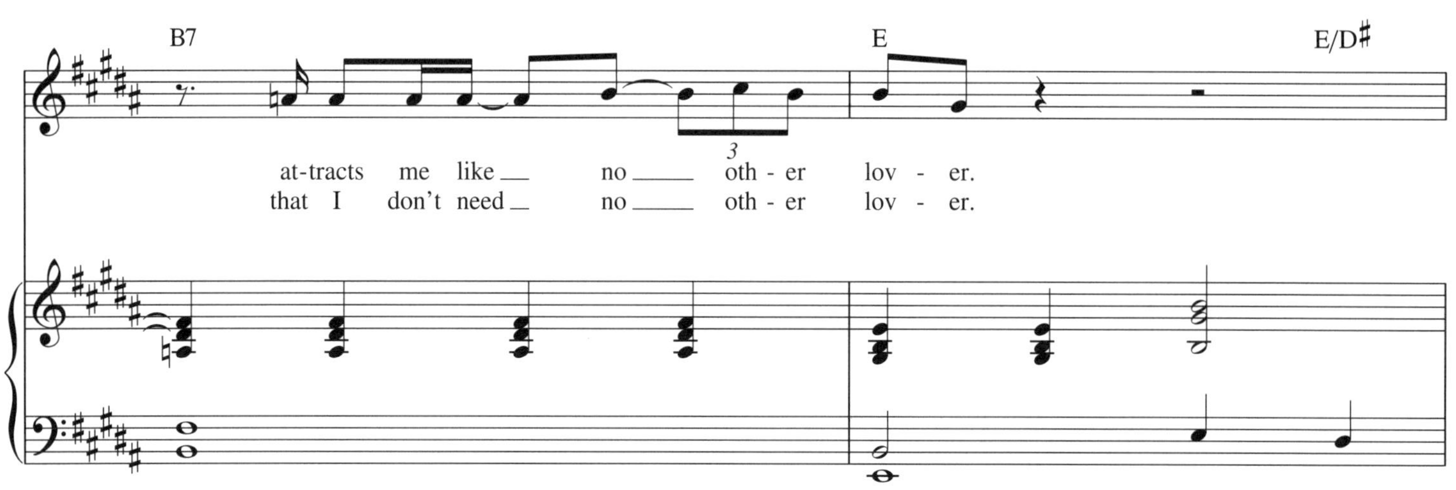

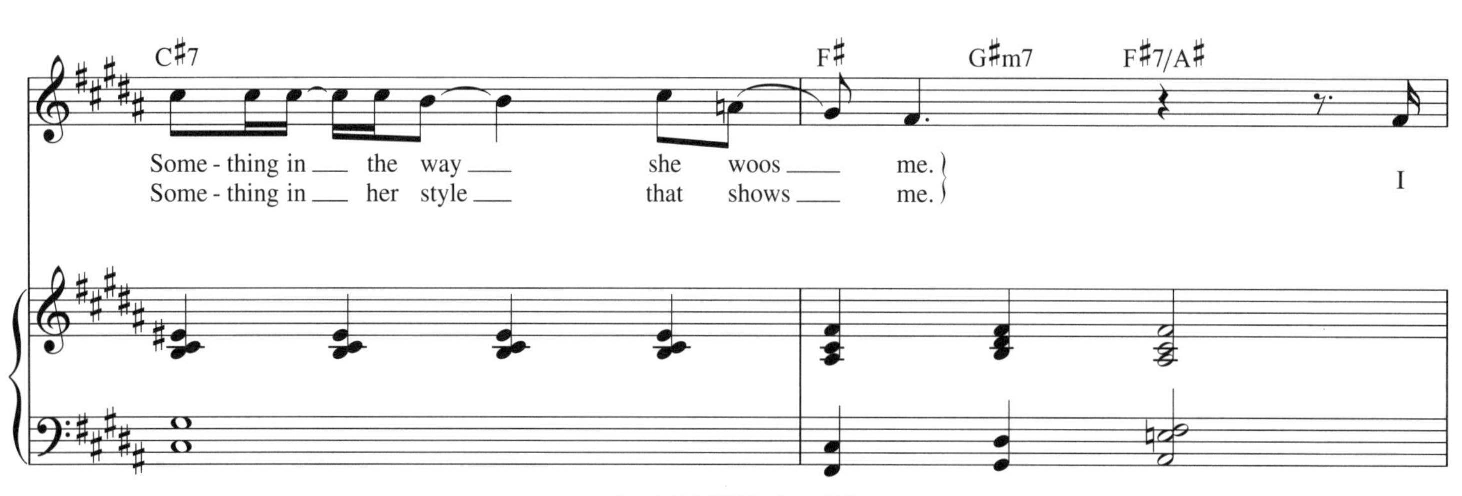

G♯m
G♯m(maj7)
G♯m7
C♯7
don't wan-na leave her now.
You know I be-lieve, and how.
1
2
E
D
F♯7/C♯
E
D
F♯7/C♯
A♭
Cm/G
You're ask - ing me, will my love
Fm
A♭/E♭
D♭
G♭
grow?
I don't know,
I don't

A♭
Cm/G
know.
You stick a - round, now it may
Fm
A♭/E♭
D♭
G♭
show.
I don't know,
I don't
B
B
know.
Bmaj7
B7
E
E/D♯

C♯7
F♯
G♯m7
F♯7/A♯

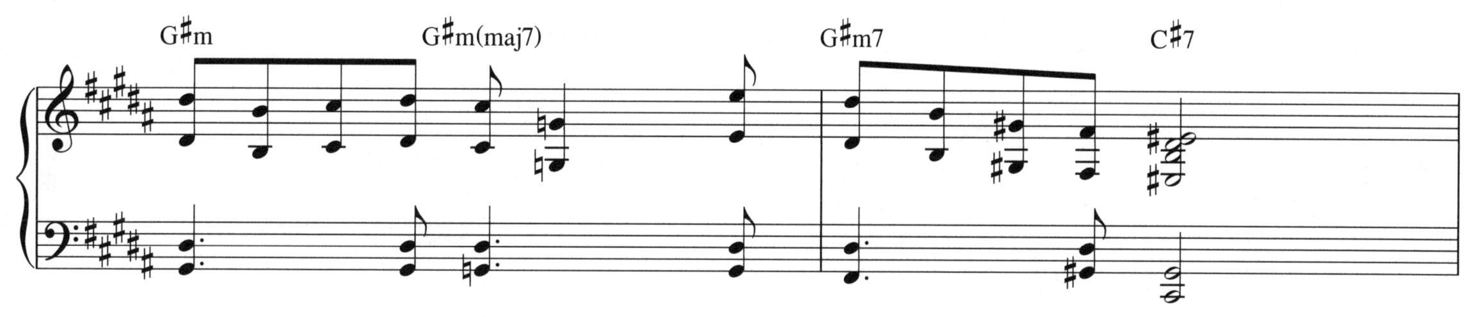
G♯m
G♯m(maj7)
G♯m7
C♯7

E
D
F♯7/C♯
B
Some - thing in ___ the way, ___ she knows, ___

Bmaj7
B7
and all I have ___ to do is

E
E/D♯
C♯7
think of her.
Some-thing in the things she
F♯
G♯m7
F♯7/A♯
G♯m
G♯m(maj7)
shows me.
I don't wan-na leave her now; you
G♯m7
C♯7
E
D
F♯7/C♯
know I be-lieve, and how.
G♯
E
D
F♯7/C♯
B
rit.

STRAWBERRY FIELDS FOREVER

Words and Music by JOHN LENNON
and PAUL McCARTNEY

Eb
Bb
F
Am/E
Straw - ber - ry Fields for - ev - er.
Liv - ing is eas - y with
Adim/Eb
Gm
F(add4)
Eb
Gm
F
eyes closed,
mis - un - der-stand-ing all you see.
Eb
F
Bb
Bb/A
Gm
Gm/F
It's get - ting hard to be some - one, but it all works out,
Eb
F
Eb
Bb
it does - n't mat - ter much to me.

Fm
Let me take you down, 'cause I'm go - ing to Straw - ber - ry
G7
Fields. Noth - ing is real, and
8vb
E♭
G
E♭
noth - ing to get hung a - bout. Straw - ber - ry Fields for -
B♭
F
Am/E
ev - er. Al - ways, no, some - times
Ped.

Adim/E♭
Gm
Gm/F
think it's me,
but you know, I know when it's a dream.
E♭
Gm
F
E♭
F
I think I know, I mean a
B♭
Gm
Gm/F
E♭
F
yes, but it's all wrong.
That is, I think I disa-
E♭
B♭
gree.
Let me take you down,

Fm
'cause I'm go - ing to Straw - ber - ry
G7
Fields. Noth - ing is real, and
E♭ F G E♭
noth - ing to get hung a - bout. Straw - ber - ry fields for -
B♭ Gm E♭ B♭
ev - er. Straw - ber - ry fields for - ev - er.

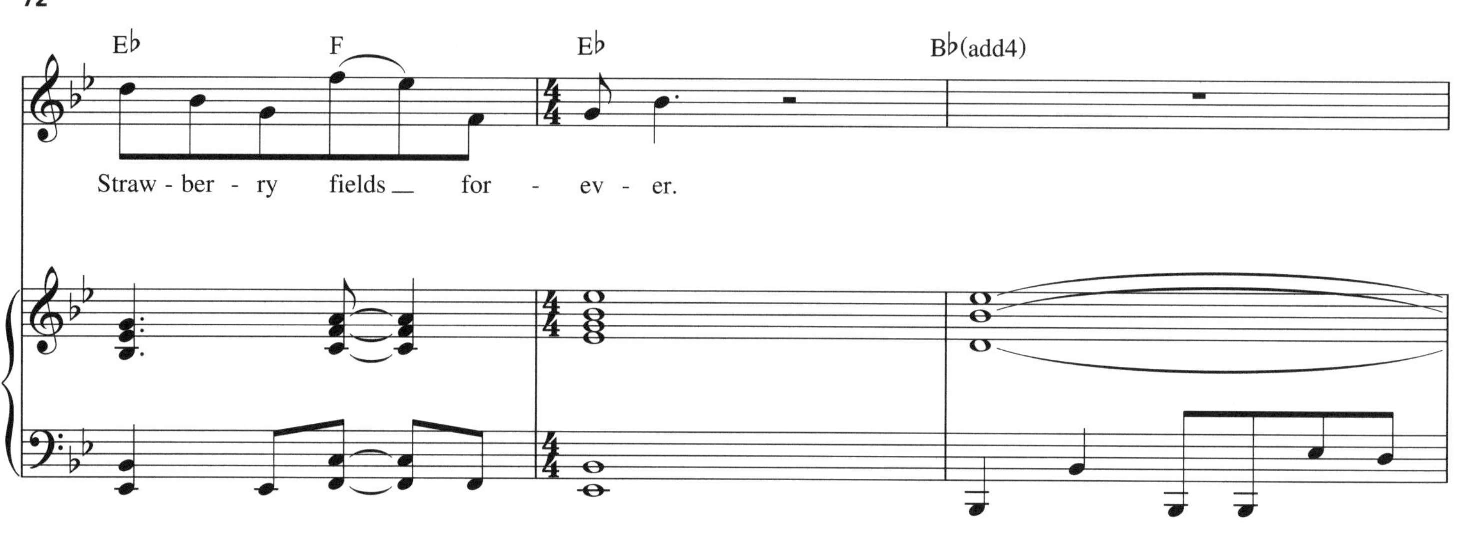
E♭
F
E♭
B♭(add4)
Straw - ber - ry fields __ for - ev - er.

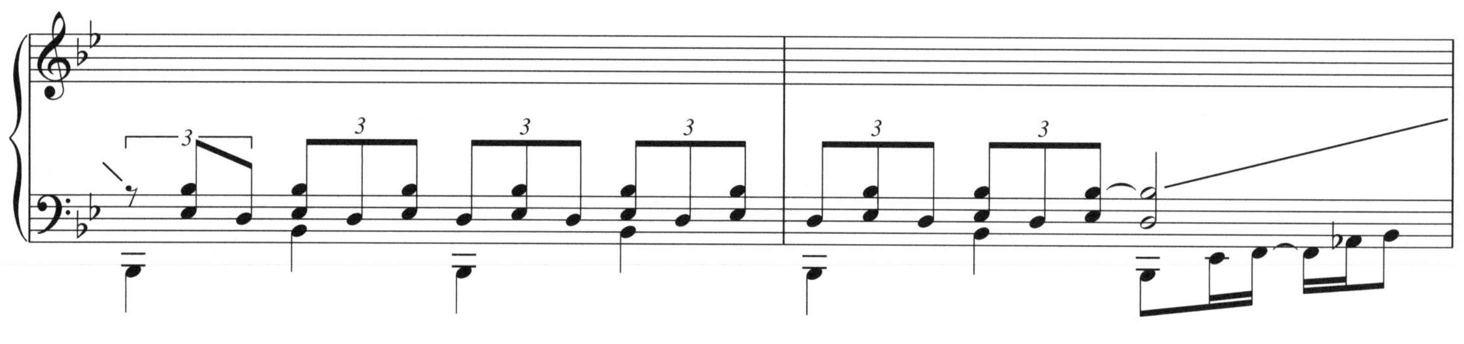

Ped.

REVOLUTION

Words and Music by JOHN LENNON
and PAUL McCARTNEY

tell me that it's ev - o - lu - tion, well,
tell me it's the in - sti - tu - tion, well,
E♭5
you know
you know
we all wan - na change the
you bet - ter free your mind in -
F5
world.
stead.
C
But when you talk a - bout de -
But if you go car - ry - ing pic - tures of
F7
struc - tion,
Chair - man Mao,
C
don't you know that you can
you ain't gon - na make it with an - y - one

Ab Bbsus G5
Fsus
count me out?
an - y - how.
Don't you know, it's gon - na be
Bb
Eb5
all right,
you know it's gon - na be
Bb
Eb5
all right,
you know it's gon - na be
Bb
Eb5
all right.
1
F7(no3rd)

2

F7(no3rd)

You All right,

Bb5 Ebsus2 Bb5

all right, all right, all right,

Ebsus2 Bb5 Ebsus2

all right, so right, so

Bb5 Fm Ab5 Fm N.C.

right.

ACROSS THE UNIVERSE

Words and Music by JOHN LENNON
and PAUL McCARTNEY

Em7
Gm(add♯4)
D5
sess - ing and ca - ress - ing me.
Jai gu - ru de -
- va,
N.C.
om.
A7
Noth - ing's gon - na change my world.
G
D
Noth - ing's gon - na change my world.
D
Bm
F♯m
Im - a - ges of brok - en light which dance be - fore me like a mil - lion eyes,

Em7
A7
they call me on and on across the u - ni - verse.

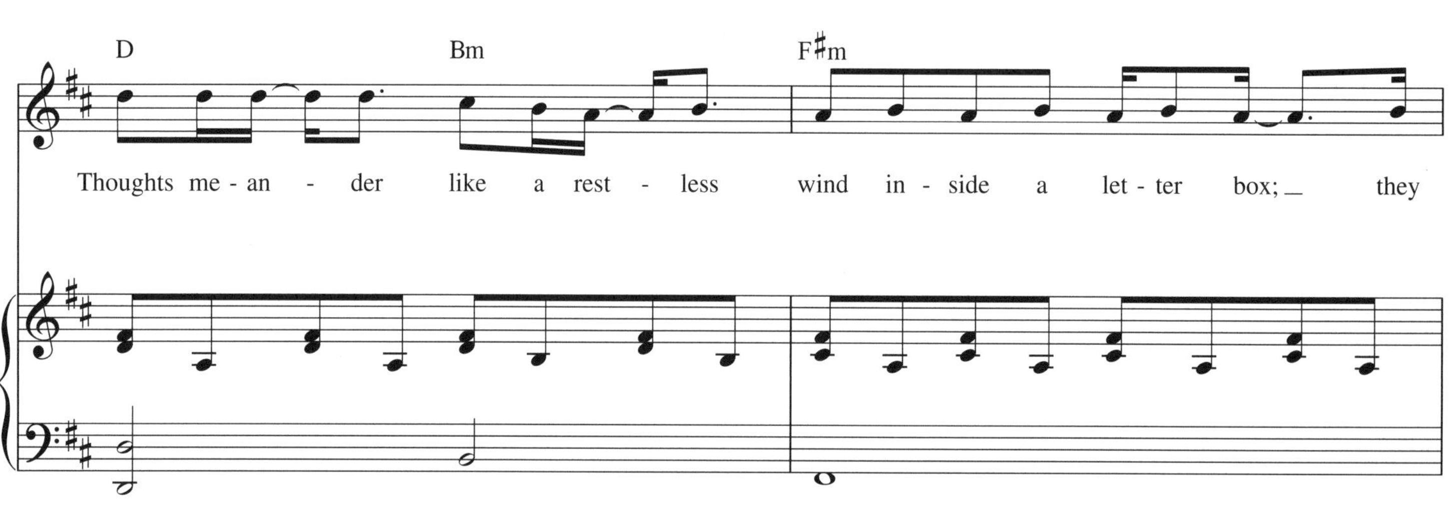
D
Bm
F♯m
Thoughts me - an - der like a rest - less wind in - side a let - ter box; they

Em7
A7
tum - ble blind - ly as they make their way a - cross the u - ni - verse.

D5
N.C.

A7
Noth - ing's gon - na change my world.
G
Noth - ing's gon - na change my world.
1-3
D
4
D
D5
(Jai gu - ru de -
1-3
- va,
4
- va,
D/F♯
om.)

BLACKBIRD

Words and Music by JOHN LENNON
and PAUL McCARTNEY

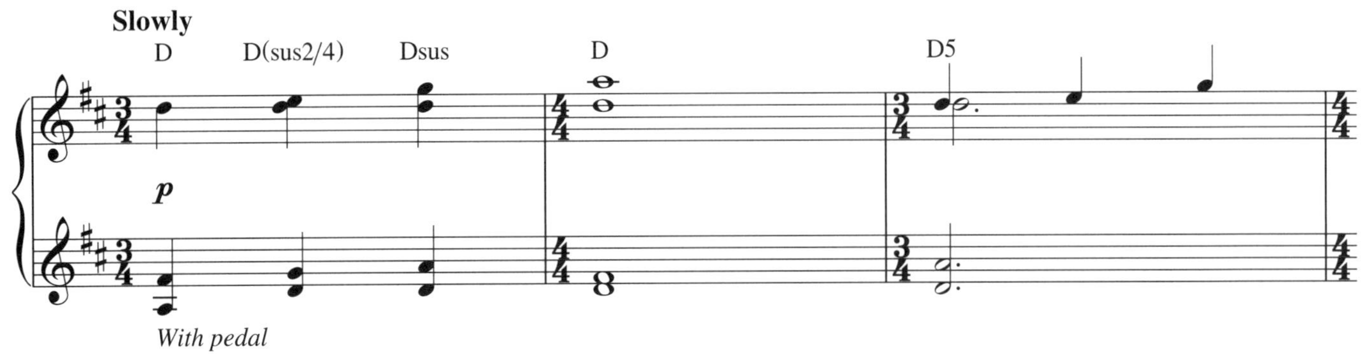

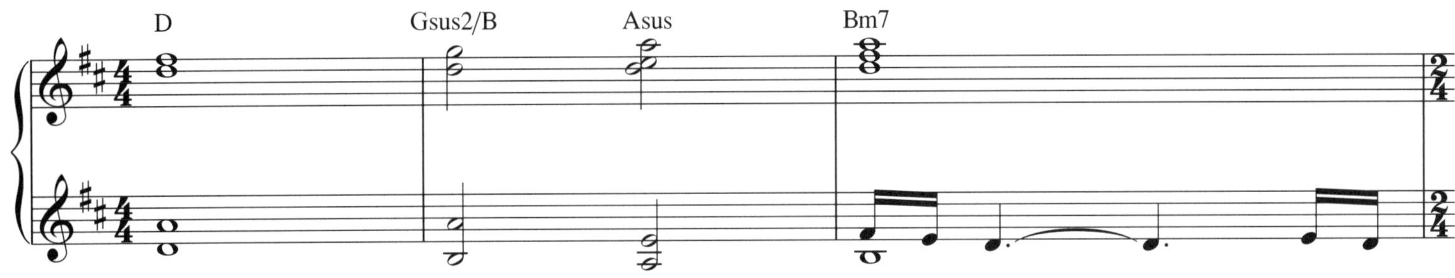

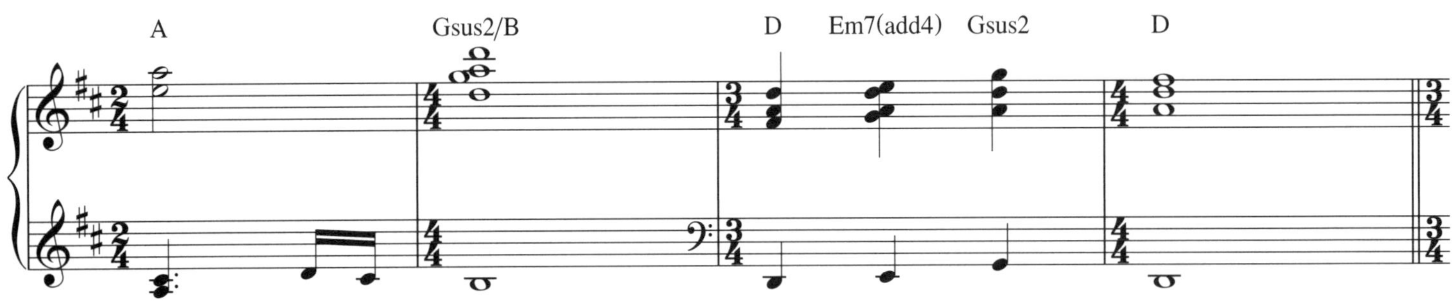

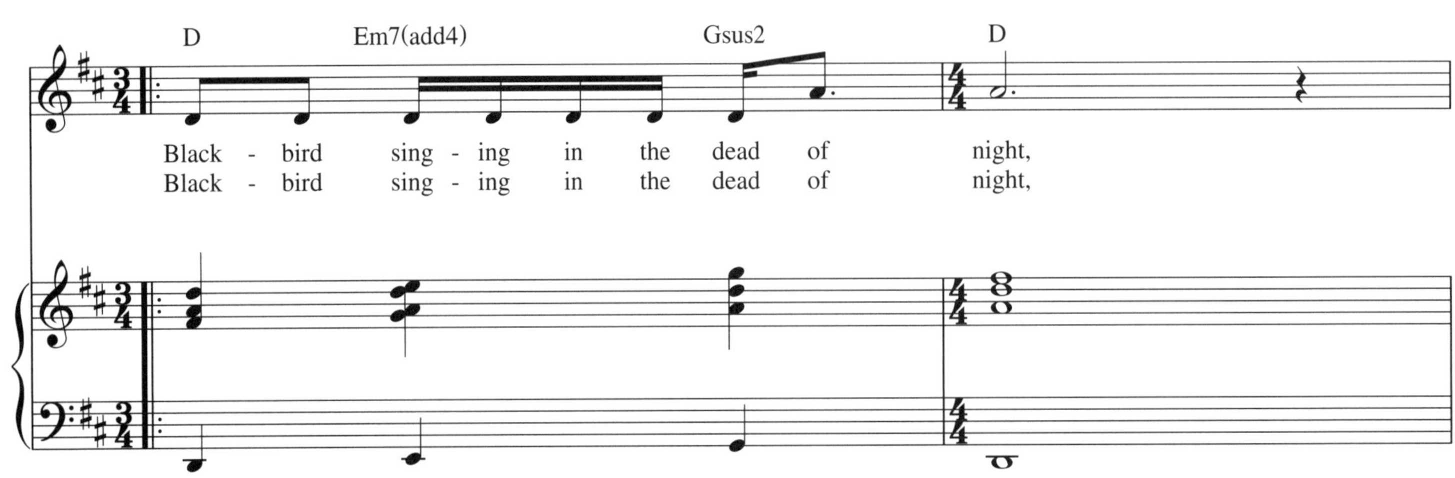

G(add2)
Asus
Bm
take these brok - en wings _ and learn _ to fly. ___
take these sunk - en eyes ___ and learn _ to see. ___
A
Gsus2
D5
E7
All your ___ life, you were on - ly wait - ing ___ for this
All your ___ life, you were on - ly wait - ing ___ for this
1
2
G5
D
Em7(add4)
Gsus2
D
G5
mo - ment to a - rise. ___
mo - ment to be free. _
D
Fsus2
Csus2/E
G5
___ Black - bird, ___ fly.

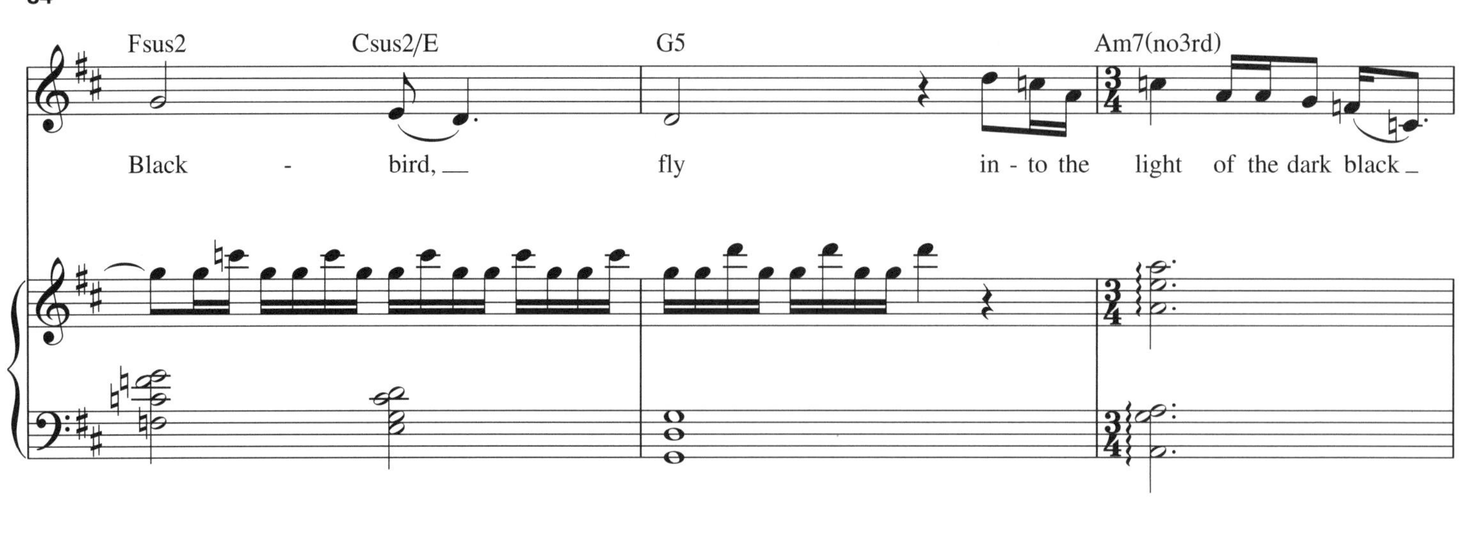
Fsus2
Csus2/E
G5
Am7(no3rd)
Black - bird, fly into the light of the dark black

D
Em7(add4)
Gsus2
D
G(add2)
Asus
Bm
night.

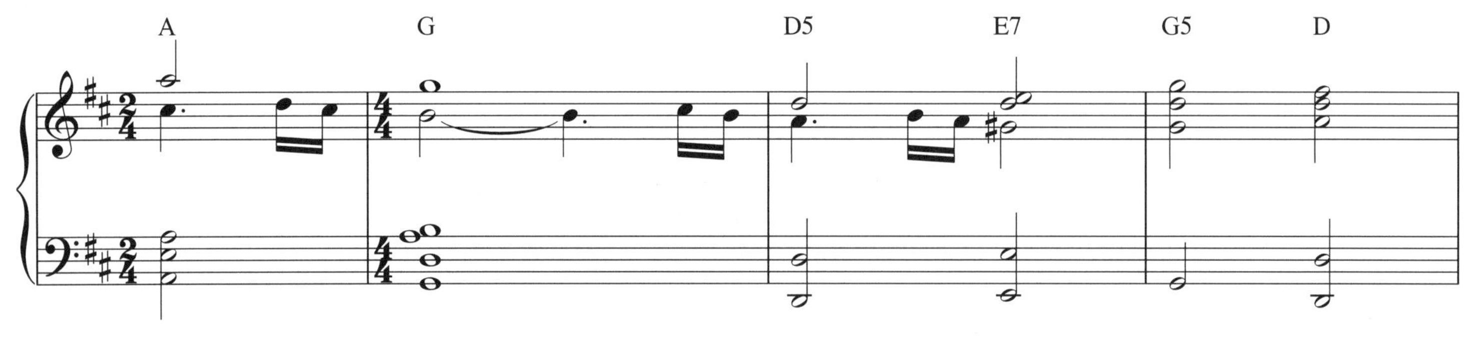
A
G
D5
E7
G5
D

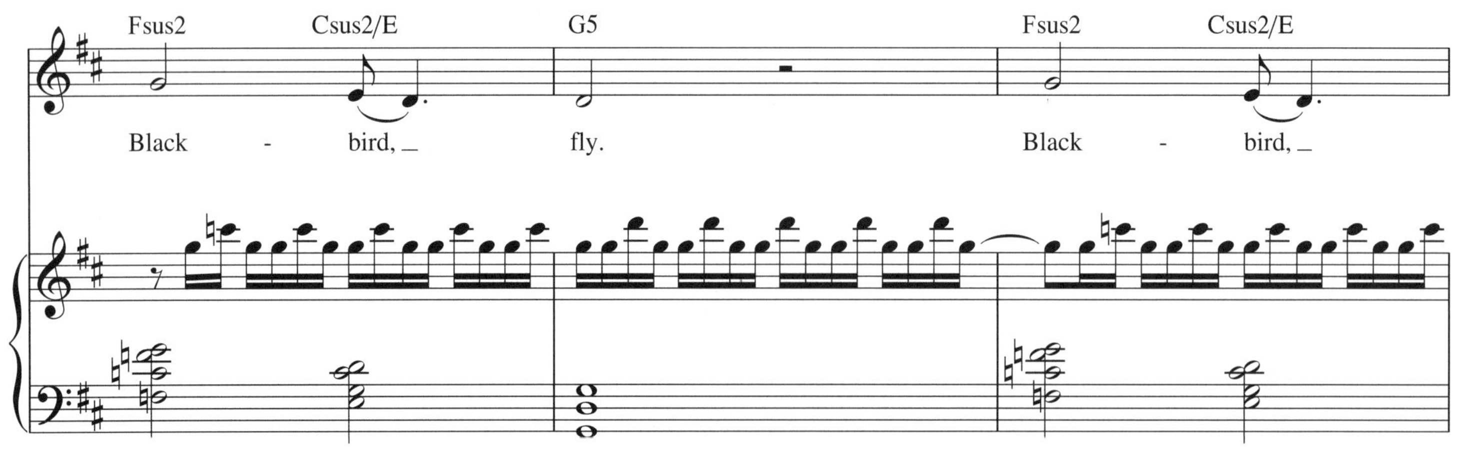
Fsus2
Csus2/E
G5
Fsus2
Csus2/E
Black - bird, fly. Black - bird,

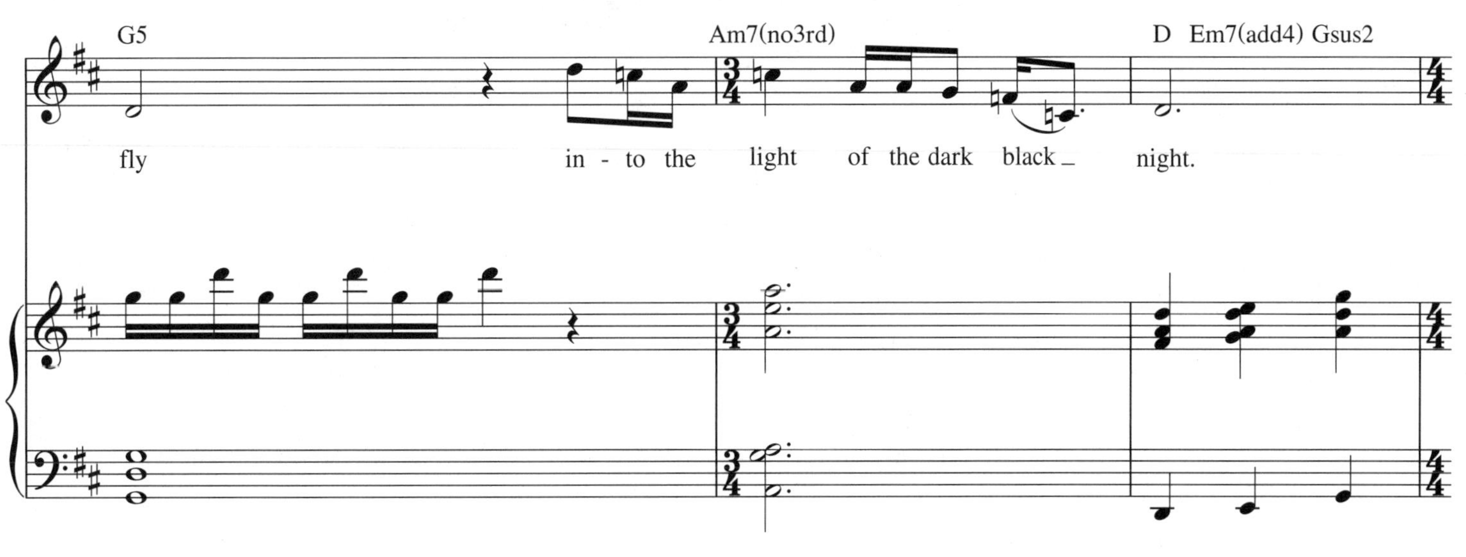
G5
Am7(no3rd)
D Em7(add4) Gsus2
fly in - to the light of the dark black_ night.

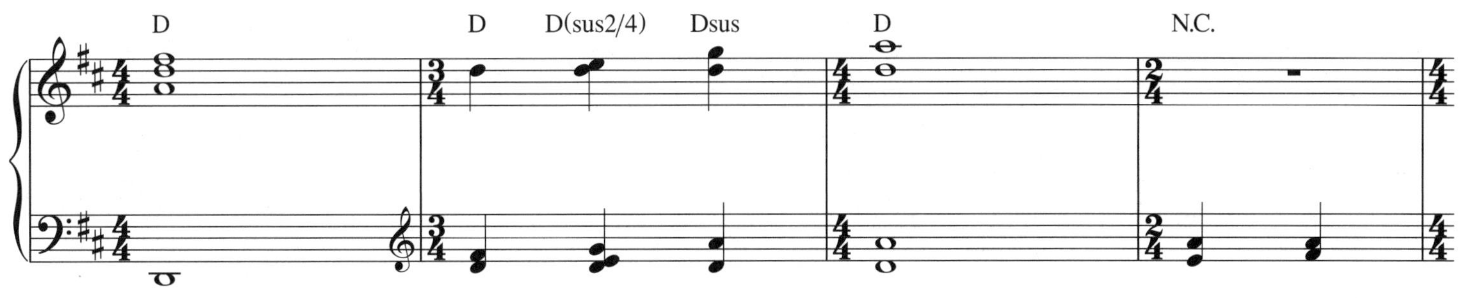
D
D D(sus2/4) Dsus
D
N.C.

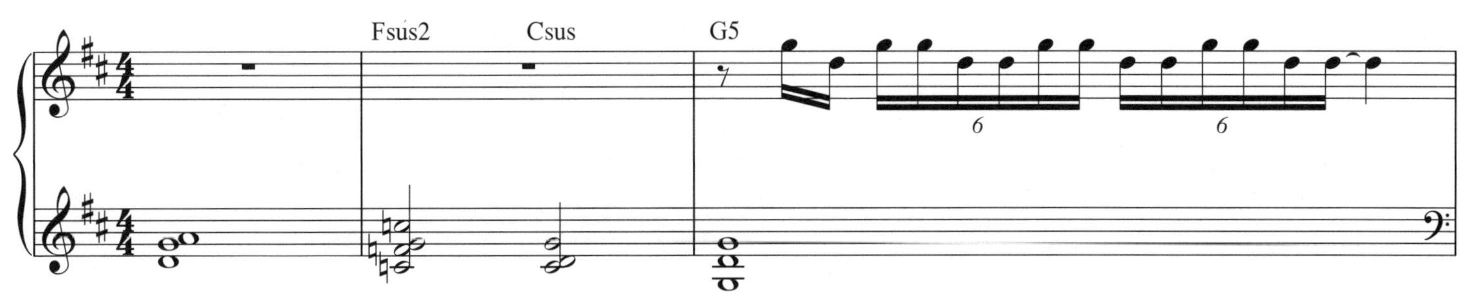
Fsus2 Csus
G5
6
6

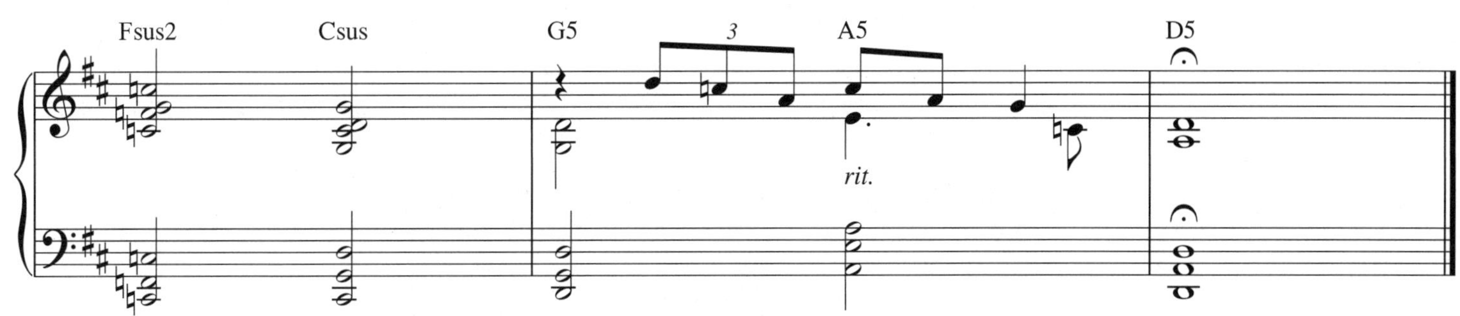
Fsus2 Csus
G5
3
A5
D5
rit.

HEY JUDE

Words and Music by JOHN LENNON
and PAUL McCARTNEY

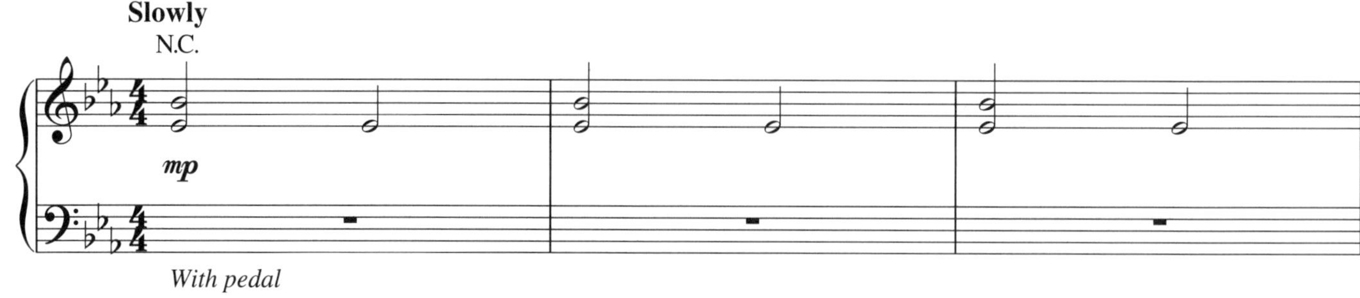

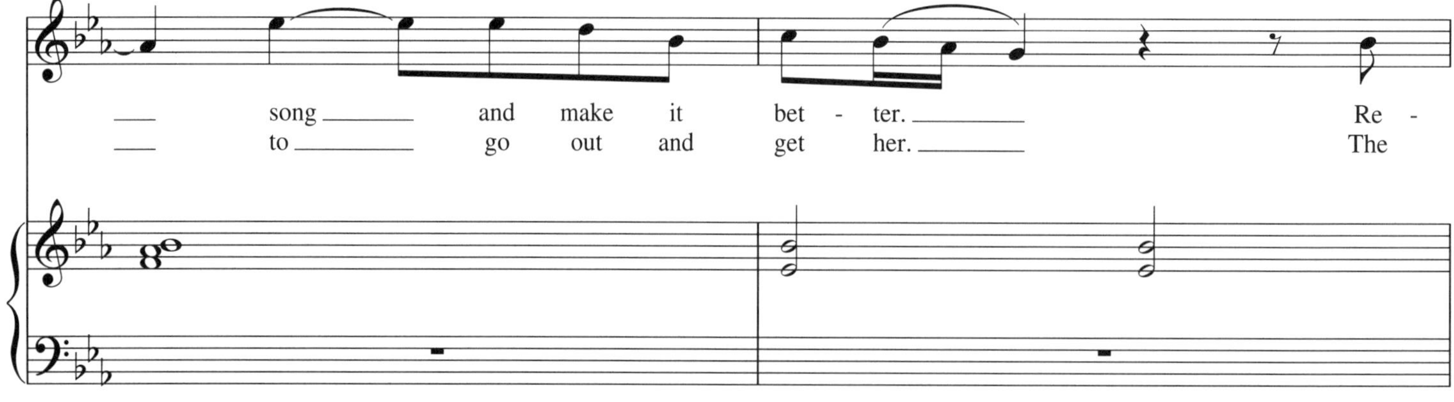

to make it bet - ter.
Hey
2
A♭
min - ute you let her un - der your
E♭
skin, then you be - gin
B♭7
to make it bet - ter.
E♭
E♭7
And an - y time you feel the pain,
A♭
hey Jude,
Cm/G
re - frain.

Fm
Ab/Eb
Bb7/D
Bb7
Don't car - ry the world upon your
Eb
Eb7
shoul - ders.
For well you know that it's a fool
Ab
Cm/G
Fm
Ab/Eb
Bb7
Bb7/C
Bb7/D
who plays it cool by mak - ing his world a lit - tle cold -
Eb
Eb7
Bb7
- er.
Na na na na na na na na na.

N.C.
Eb
3
Hey Jude, don't let me
Bb
Bb7
down; you have found her, now go and
Eb
Ab
get her. Re - mem - ber to let her in - to your
(Let it out and let it in.)
Eb
Bb7
Eb
heart; then you can start to make it bet - ter, bet - ter, bet - ter, bet - ter,

N.C.
E♭
D♭
bet - ter, bet - ter, ow!
(Na na na na na na na,
Lead vocal ad lib.
Repeat ad lib.
A♭
E♭
na na na na, hey Jude.
Last Time
E♭
E♭
D♭
A♭
E♭

DON'T LET ME DOWN

Words and Music by JOHN LENNON
and PAUL McCARTNEY

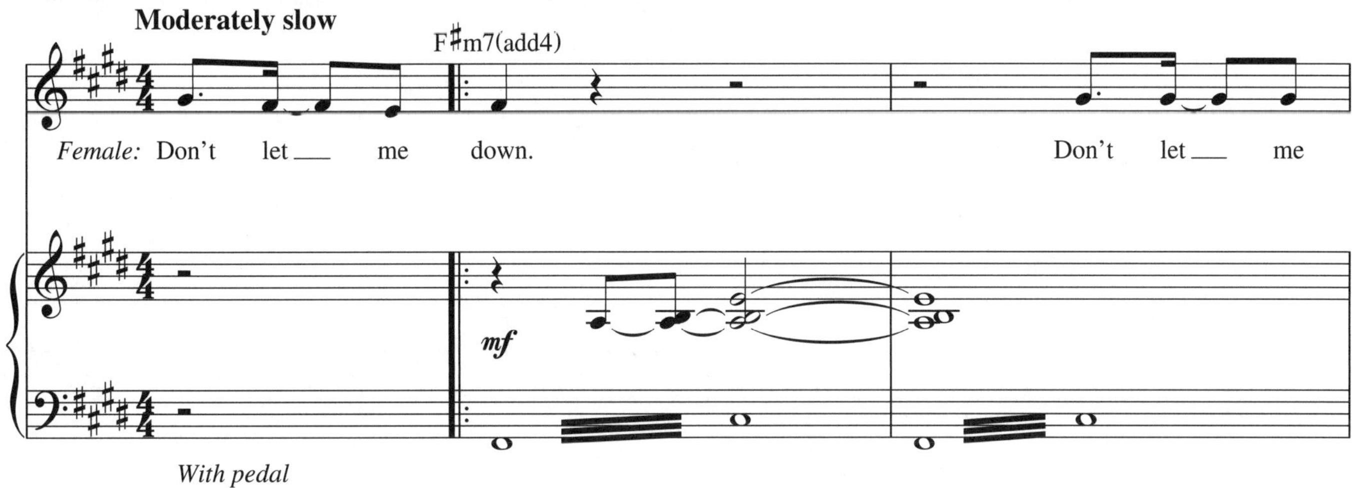

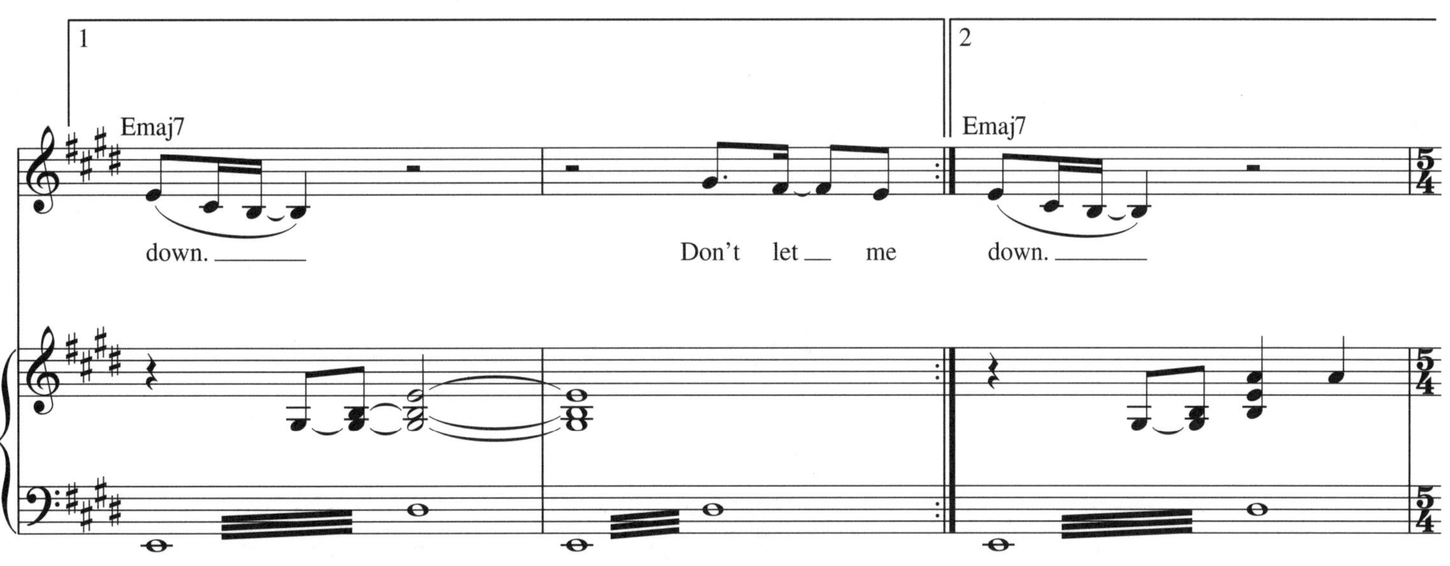

E6
yes, he does.
F♯m7(add4)
Male: And if some-bod-y loved me like she do me, ooh, she do
E6
me, yeah, she does.
F♯m
Both: Don't let me down.

F♯m7
Don't let __ me down. __
E
Don't let __ me
F♯m
down.
F♯m7
Don't let __ me
E
down. __
Female: Oh, I'm in love for the first __ time.
Don't you know, it's gon - na last. __
B/F♯

B7
Male: It's the love that lasts for - ev - er;
Both: it's the love that has no past.
E
Don't let me
F♯m
down.
F♯m7
Don't let me
E
down.
Don't let me

F♯m
F♯m7
E
down.
Don't let me down.
Bkgrd.: (Don't let me
Am
down.
Lead vocal ad lib.
Don't let me down.
G
Don't let me
Am
down.
Don't let me

G
Am
down.
Don't you let me down.
Don't let ___ me down. ___ Nev - er,
nev - er, nev - er let ___ me down.
Don't let ___ me down.) ___
rit.

ALL YOU NEED IS LOVE

Words and Music by JOHN LENNON
and PAUL McCARTNEY

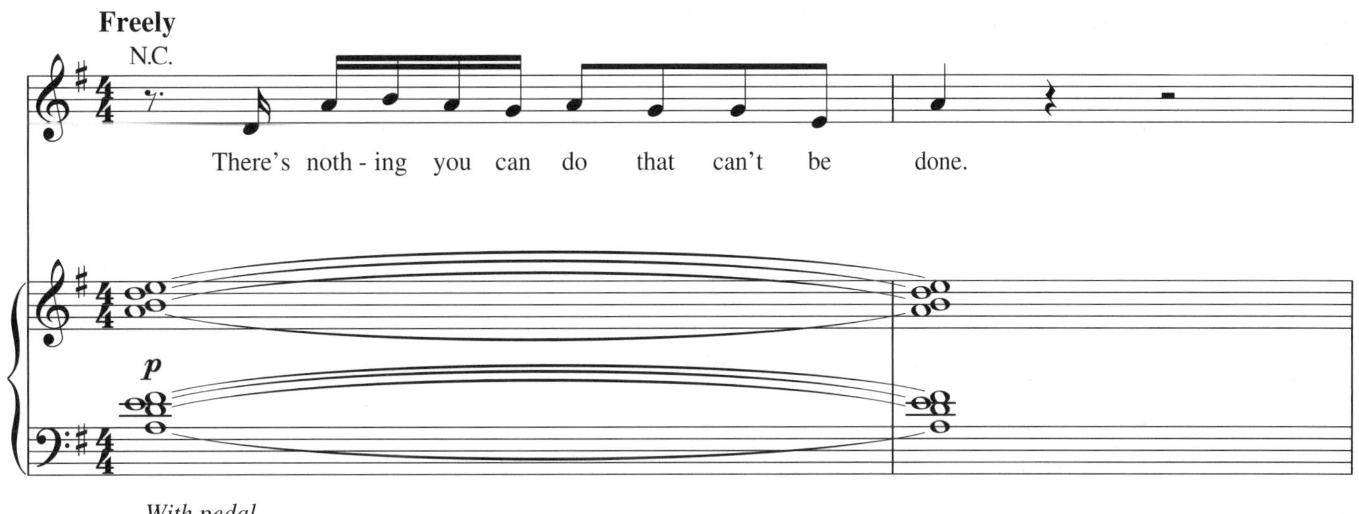

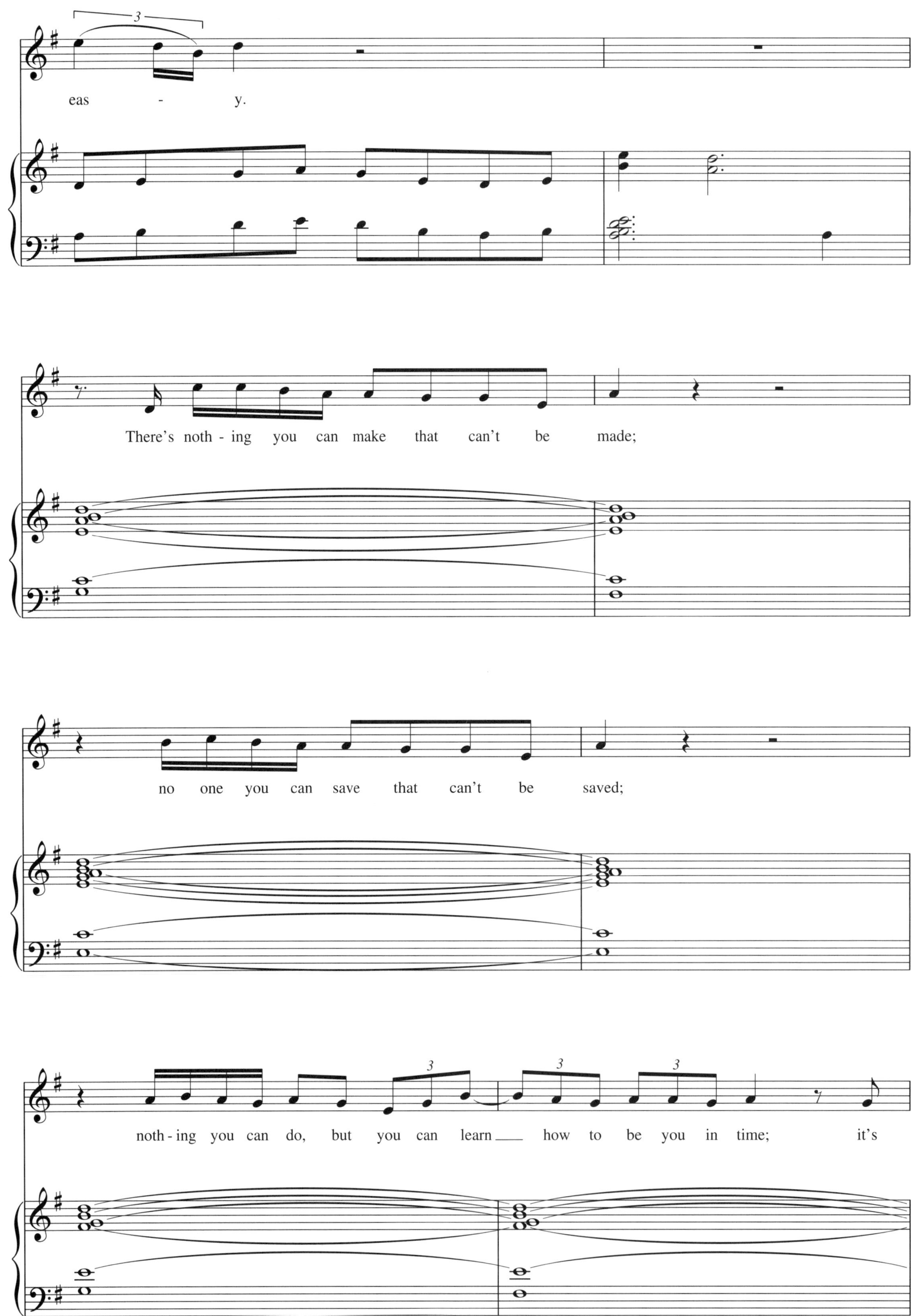
3
eas - y.
There's noth - ing you can make that can't be made;
no one you can save that can't be saved;
3
3
3
noth - ing you can do, but you can learn how to be you in time; it's

eas - y.
All you need is love.
All you need is love.
All you need is love,
love;
love is all you need.
G
D/F♯
Em7(add4)
(Love,
love,
love.)

G
D/F♯
Em7(add4)
There's noth - ing you can know that can't be known;
(Love, love, love.)
G
D/F♯
Em7
noth - ing you can see that is - n't shown;
(Love, love, love.)
D
no - where you can be that is - n't where you're meant to be; it's
Easy Shuffle
D5
D5/C
N.C.
eas - y.
mf

G
A7
D5
All you need is love.
G
A7
D5
G
B7
All you need is love.
All you need is love,
Em
G/D
love;
1
C
D5
love is all you need.
2
C
D5
G
A7
love is all you need.
All you need is love.

D5
G
A7
D5
All you need is love.
G
B7
Em
G/D
All you need is love,
love;
C
D5
(love is all you need.)
G5
D5
Vocal 1: Love is all you need.
Vocal 2: Love is all
E5
Love is all you need.
you need.
Love is all you need.
G5
D5
Love is all you need.
Love is all

E5 G5 D5
Love is all you need.
you need. Love is all you need. Love is all
E5 C5 G5 D5
Love is all you need. Love is all you need.
you need. Love is all you need.
E5 C5 G B7
Both: Love is all you need. All you need is love,
Em G/D C D5 G5
love; love is all you need.
rit.

WHY DON'T WE DO IT IN THE ROAD

Words and Music by JOHN LENNON
and PAUL McCARTNEY

G5
Bb5
G5
F5
Eb5
No one will be watch - ing us; why
(8vb)
Bb5
F(add#9)
don't we do it in the road?
1
Why don't we do it in the road?
8vb
2
G5
Bb5
G5
F5
Eb5
I said, no one will be watch - ing us; why
(8vb)
Bb5
F(add#9)
don't we do it in the road.

LUCY IN THE SKY WITH DIAMONDS

Words and Music by JOHN LENNON
and PAUL McCARTNEY

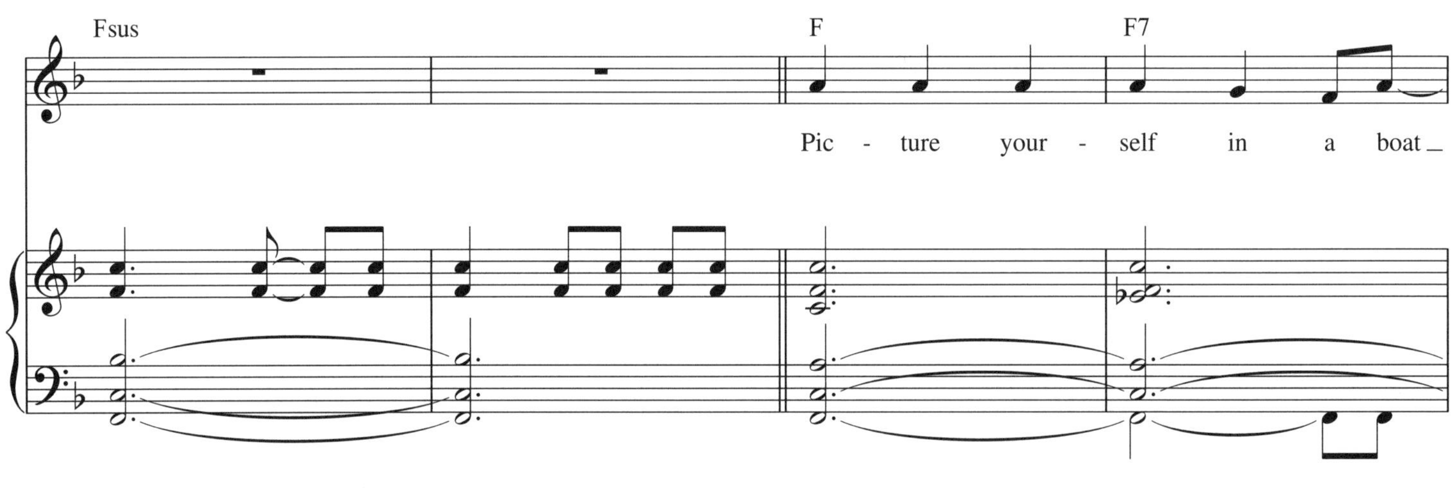

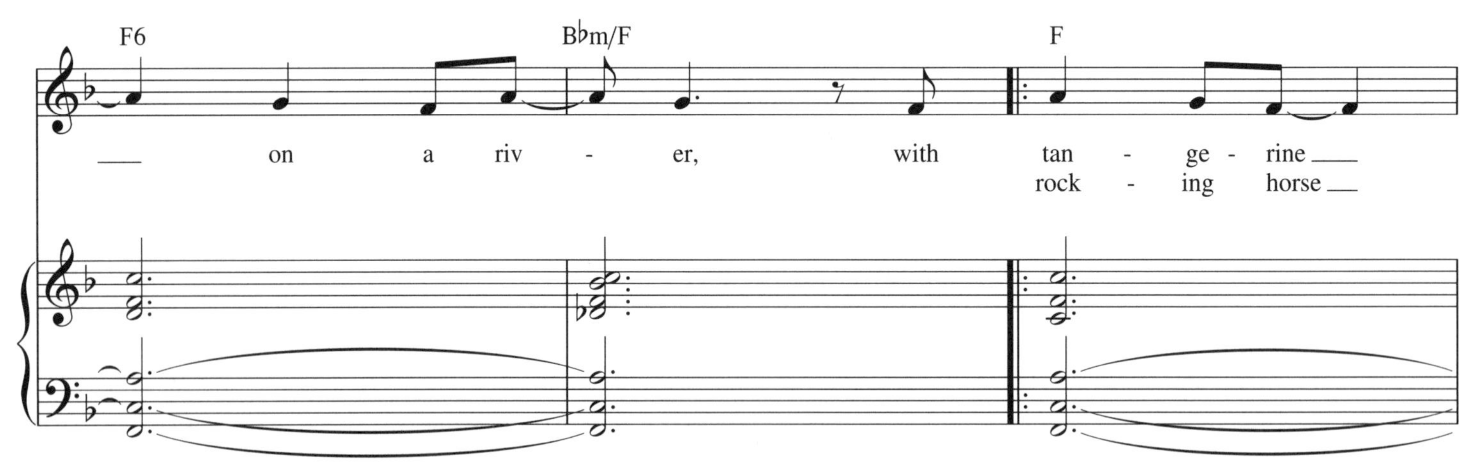

F7 F6 B♭m/F

trees and mar - ma - lade skies.
peo - ple eat marsh - mal - low pies.

F F7 F6

Some - bod - y calls you; you an - swer quite
Ev - 'ry - one smiles as you drift past the

B♭m/F F F7

slow - ly, the girl with ka - lei - do - scope
flow - ers that grow so in - cred - i - bly

F6 B♭m/F B♭m B♭m/A♭

eyes.
high.

G♭
A♭sus2
Cel - lo - phane flow - ers of yel - low and
News - pa - per tax - is ap - pear on the
D♭6
G♭
green, tow - er - ing o - ver your head.
shore, wait - ing to take you a - way.
A♭sus2
E♭
Look for the girl with the sun in her
Climb in the back with your head in the
(𝅗𝅥. = 𝅗𝅥)
B♭(add4)
E♭
A♭
eyes, and she's gone.
clouds, and you're gone.
Lu - cy in the sky with

B♭sus
E♭
A♭
B♭sus
dia - monds.
Lu - cy in the sky with dia - monds.
E♭
A♭
B♭
1
Lu - cy in the sky with dia - monds.
(Oh.)
(𝅗𝅥 = 𝅗𝅥.)
F
F7
F6
Fol - low her down to a bridge by a foun -
B♭m/F
2
(𝅗𝅥 = 𝅗𝅥.)
F
- tain where (Oh.)
Pic - ture your -

F7
F6
B♭m/F
self on a train in a sta - tion with
F
F7
F6
plas - ti - cine por - ters, with look - ing glass ties.
B♭m/F
F
Sud - den - ly some -
F7
F6
B♭m/F
F
- one is there at the turn - stile; the girl with ka - lei -

F7
B♭sus/F
B♭m/F
- do-scope eyes.
(♩. = 𝅗𝅥)
E♭/G
A♭6/9
B♭sus
F7sus/C
(1., 2.) Lu - cy in the sky with dia - monds.
(3.) *Instrumental*
B♭sus
B♭sus/A♭
E♭/G
F7sus
E♭sus2
Lu - cy in the sky with dia - monds.
E♭/G
A♭6/9
B♭sus
Lu - cy in the sky with dia - monds.

B♭
A♭6
Play 3 times
E♭
A♭
(Oh.)
Lu - cy in the sky with
B♭sus
E♭
A♭
dia - monds.
Lu - cy in the sky with
B♭sus
E♭
A♭
dia - monds.
Lu - cy in the sky with
B♭
F7(no3rd)
dia - monds.
(Oh.)